By Grace Alone

By Grace Alone

Forgiveness
for Everyone,
for Everything,
for Evermore

J. HAROLD ELLENS

WIPF & STOCK · Eugene, Oregon

BY GRACE ALONE
Forgiveness for Everyone, for Everything, for Evermore

Copyright © 2013 J. Harold Ellens. All rights reserved. Except for brief quotations in critical publications or reviews, no part of this book may be reproduced in any manner without prior written permission from the publisher. Write: Permissions. Wipf and Stock Publishers, 199 W. 8th Ave., Suite 3, Eugene, OR 97401.

Wipf & Stock
An Imprint of Wipf and Stock Publishers
199 W. 8th Ave., Suite 3
Eugene, OR 97401

www.wipfandstock.com

ISBN 13: 978-1-62564-148-9

Manufactured in the U.S.A.

This volume of sermons is dedicated to the loving memory of three of my brothers, Stanley Ellens, Gordon Henry Ellens, and Gordon John Ellens, who have preceded me into the eternal world where faith becomes sight and hope is fulfilled. Gordon Henry died in childhood. Stanley and Gordon John lived decisive lives as towering leaders in the church and the world. They all died untimely deaths, but ready for the life transcendent and eternal. They knew with deep personal assurance that by grace alone they were loved unconditionally and forgiven for everything forevermore.

Contents

Foreword by Virginia Ingram | ix
Introduction | ix

SERMON ONE
Grace When Least Expected | 1
—Micah 7:18–20; Ephesians 4

SERMON TWO
Love Has Good Manners | 8
—1 Corinthians 13:4–6

SERMON THREE
God and Beauty | 14
—Genesis 1:1, 1:31; Psalm 19:1–4

SERMON FOUR
He Who Has the Most Toys Wins | 21
—Psalm 107:8–9; Luke 12:13–21

SERMON FIVE
Mercy and Not Sacrifice: A Stewardship Sermon | 25
—Matthew 9:1–13

SERMON SIX
A Usable Future | 29
—Matthew 16:13–19

SERMON SEVEN
As a Dying Man | 34
—1 Corinthians 9:16–18

SERMON EIGHT
By the Skin of Our Teeth | 44
—Romans 12:2, 12:21

SERMON NINE
A Weeping God? | 50
—John 11:35

SERMON TEN
The Cross as Christian Symbol | 56
—Matthew 4:1–2, 4:8–9; 16:24–26; 1 Corinthians 1:17–18, 1:21–25

SERMON ELEVEN
The Laughing Christ | 64
—Hosea 1:1–3:1b

SERMON TWELVE
When God Moves In | 70
—Revelation 21:1–8

SERMON THIRTEEN
The Purposes of Prayer | 77
—Matthew 6:1–13

SERMON FOURTEEN
Do You Fear God? | 83
—Mark 1:1–4, 1:14–15, 1:21–28

SERMON FIFTEEN
Is Jesus Really God? | 91
—John 1:1–14; Mark 15:34–39

SERMON SIXTEEN
For God's Pleasure and Purposes | 97
—Psalm 149:1–6a; Numbers 6:24–26

SERMON SEVENTEEN
Be Transformed | 101
—Romans 12:1–13

SERMON EIGHTEEN
Christians as Theologians | 106
—Ezra 7:6–10; Matthew 22:15–17a

SERMON NINETEEN
God's Mountain | 110
—Psalm 48; 2 Sam 5:1–5, 5:9–10

SERMON TWENTY
God Rested | 115
—Genesis 1–2:3; Exodus 20:8–11; Hebrews 4:4, 4:9–11a

SERMON TWENTY ONE
A Snake in the Desert | 120
—Numbers 21:4–9; John 3:14–21, 8:28, 12:32–34; Ephesians 2:4–10

SERMON TWENTY TWO
Minister's Mandate, Congregation's Call | 125
—Matthew 16:13b–18.

SERMON TWENTY THREE
Christian Olympics | 129
—Hebrews 12:1–2a

SERMON TWENTY FOUR
The Empty God | 135
—Philippians 2:5–11

SERMON TWENTY FIVE
Spirituality Right Side Up | 139
—Ephesians 2:4–10

SERMON TWENTY SIX
Spirituality Upside Down or Inside Out | 145
—James 1:1—4:20

SERMON TWENTY SEVEN
So What, Operationally | 151
—Revelation 5:11–14

Conclusion | 155
Index | 157

Foreword

IN THE FIRST YEAR of my undergraduate degree I met Professor J. Harold Ellens at the Auckland meeting of the Society of Biblical Literature. In a general introduction to the section he was chairing, *Psychological Hermeneutics of Biblical Themes and Texts,* I said that I did not have a special discipline like the other members of the group, but that I was keen to learn. Not missing an opportunity to spread God's word, Dr. Ellens responded by saying that it was his life's work to teach, and to empower young scholars to achieve the fulfillment of their potential. As they say, the rest is history. Dr. Ellens has been my mentor and dear friend for some time now. I often say to him that our friendship is the defining relationship in my life, quite simply because his compassionate nature has touched me and guided me through my own transformation from a scared young woman to a confident and hopeful one.

On reflection, I realize that Dr. Ellens has taught me much more than what I have learned in reading academic texts. When I first met him my engagement with theology was purely intellectual, and I could hide from experiencing God's love in my life by burying myself in technical books and writing essays. Yet the most awesome thing about his ministry of grace—grace which is radical, universal, and unconditional—is that it refuses to sit in our heads as a clever idea, but rather transforms us into psycho-spiritually healthy individuals. Suffice it to say that Dr. Ellens' theology became part of me and changed my life. Thereby, I learned that theology for him is a lived experience.

As an aside, I find it interesting to note that his faith statement of God's unconditional love to us, a love that is not guaranteed by good works, comes forth from a person who lives his life completely oriented to serving God "in the trenches," as he says. For example, you can find in print

Foreword

many examples of Dr. Ellens spontaneously perceiving and following an intimation of the spirit: where he has encouraged a woman who is struggling alone with two children in McDonalds, counseled a suicidal airline checking agent, and cared for bereaved soldiers. What is not in print is the ministry of grace he tirelessly extends to his fellow colleagues, students, patients, parishioners, and now to you with this volume of his engaging sermons.

The sermons in this book are unique for a number of reasons. First, they have been crafted by a world recognized scholar. Second, they have been written by a psychologist who has been in practice for over half a century. Third, they have been delivered by a priest who has devoted his entire life to serving God's word. As you can see, this dear friend is a man who has learned to love God with all of his heart, mind, and soul. Moreover, because Dr. Ellens wears these different hats he is able to create addresses which are intelligent without being beyond the reach of those who listen to them, entertaining without being trite, and stimulating so that it is impossible to put this book down without considering his illumining words.

However, I think the thing that attracts me most about Dr. Ellens' writing is that he is not afraid to be vulnerable in his addresses, and he shares with his readers his own painful journey in what he calls the tragic comedy of life. For those of you who are not well versed in Greek drama that means there is always hope—hope for a better day, hope for a better life, and hope for a better world. Nonetheless Dr. Ellens acknowledges that life is messy and painful at times, even gut-wrenching, and as John F. Kennedy said, "a tragic adventure" at best. In the face of all of the difficulties life throws at us, my dear friend, Harold, is the person who is always smiling in front of us saying, "Don't give up, God loves you." I trust this vision and I have come to believe Harold's message of grace, because I know he believes it with all his heart, and lives it every day. Most recently, I know that he has suffered from major health concerns, yet he has always been resolute in his faith. Maybe there is a doctor, nurse, or patient in the hospital who needs to hear the word of God's grace, Harold has pondered, as he put his own needs in second place.

As you may have noticed there is no limit to my feelings of esteem for The Reverend Dr. J. Harold Ellens. He puts me in mind of that critical day of Latimer and Ridley, bishops and martyrs who were burned at the stake for telling the truth. As they faced their final moment Bishop Latimer said blithely to Ridley, "Play the man, Master Ridley; we shall this day light such a candle, by God's grace, in England, as I trust shall never be put out!"

Virginia Ingram
All Hallows Eve, 2012

Introduction

SERMONS ARE SUPPOSED TO be one form of what the Bible calls proclamation. Proclamation in the biblical sense means any form of communication that gets across the message of the Bible to humans who wish to hear it. Thus proclamation can take the form of drama, lectures, various types of oratory, audio-visuals, dance, mime presentations, writing, and online expressions. Sermons, however, are a specific kind of communication in which the gospel message is to be spoken, enacted, and incarnated by the preacher.

So sermons are to be proclaimed and experienced existentially, in an immediate face-to-face encounter between the preacher and the congregation. The experience is intended to be mediated by voice, body language, emotional engagement, intellectual finesse, and enactment of the message in ways that attract and inspire the congregation. Therefore, a sermon is not a lecture, seldom a formal dialogue, usually not a theater piece. Those are all desirable forms of proclamation, but they are not sermons in which the person of the preacher becomes the incarnation of the Word.

In this volume I am offering a group of written sermons. Written sermons lack the virtue of being proclaimed with obvious emotion and body language on the part of the orator/preacher. They may, nonetheless, engage the audience emotionally and intellectually if they are well crafted in felicitous language. I hope and pray that the readers of this volume will find that these sermons possess those virtues and speak well to the mind and heart.

Historically sermons in the Christian tradition have been designed mainly to address the left brain of the listener. That tendency exists, unfortunately, because it is mainly in the right brain that the kind of reflection happens that shapes our spiritual hunger and religious response. The left brain is primarily designed for linear logic and problem solving, while the

Introduction

right brain is the center of our affect, emotion, and perception of the aesthetic dimensions of the color, texture, and meaning of life as we experience it. Good preaching needs to address both dimensions of the human process of knowing, learning, and understanding.

It has been my longstanding endeavor to craft my sermons in a way that will move through the head to the heart. To do such a thing a sermon must satisfy the left brain but primarily appeal to the right brain of the hearers. I pray that in this volume it may be evident to the reader that I have in some degree succeeded in accomplishing that task.

I offer these sermons to any and all who can find them useful. Read them, use them, preach them, and make them live again in the fully incarnated form if you can. They have been developed over the 60 years of my ministry and now they belong to the Divine Spirit to be used as God will use them.

All Hallows Eve, 2012

SERMON ONE

Grace When Least Expected
—Micah 7:18–20; Ephesians 4

Who is a God like our God? He tramples our iniquities under his feet.

—Micah 7:18–19

Micah was a prophet in Israel who lived six centuries before Jesus was born. That was a bad time in ancient Israel. The Israelites claimed they were God's special people but they acted like they had gone to the devil. Their spiritual leaders accused them of many evil things. They had really forsaken their covenant relationship with God. They no longer felt the presence of the Divine Spirit in their personal or communal lives. It was impossible to tell the difference between the people of Yahweh and the worshippers of Baal, or of the idols of the other Canaanites. The Israelites had the reputation of a society radically divided between the wealthy and powerful, and the less fortunate. The rich would sell the poor for a pair of shoes, the prophets said, and the smoke of their worship services and sacrifices were a stench in God's nostrils. God hated it and the prophets incessantly harangued the people fruitlessly. It did nothing to change their behavior and call them back to the ways of God.

By Grace Alone

Micah knew that if he were to make a dent in their consciousness he would need to find a way to give the nation a swift kick in the belly, or send a message they could not forget, ignore, or cough up out of their conscience. Micah was wise and gracious. He decided to take the high road with that wicked people. He chose a positive metaphor that is both memorable and meaningful. He said, "God has cast all our sins into the depths of the sea" Later in the Bible we learn that he is referring to the sea of God's forgetfulness.

That is a memorable metaphor. I guarantee that now that I have brought it to your attention *you* will never again be able to forget it. Israel never forgot it either. It did not always influence their behavior, but when it did not it made them immensely uncomfortable. It confronted them with their real natures, but most of all it reminded them of God's covenant with their forefathers, that God would make sure humans could never sin themselves out of God's forgiving grace. Neither they nor we could squirm from God's eternal embrace. To this day the Jewish people cannot forget Micah's metaphor. It is in their scripture and in their psyches to make them and us either immensely uncomfortable, or overwhelmed with the sense of freedom in divine forgiveness.

Now, that is all well and good. It is a memorable and attention-getting metaphor. However, we need to ask ourselves what that metaphor has to do with us today. What is its meaning for the twenty-first century world? Well, this present world is socially and culturally rather chaotic. We live in a frenzy of trying to deal with our inner disorder and our outer derangement. The feeling of most humans everywhere in the world is that things are largely out-of-joint. Governments fail to achieve the decent and prosperous objectives we all need. Local societies flounder from lack of funds and greedy, unimaginative leadership. School systems come up short in educating our children in useful ideals and hopeful excitement about striving for lives of quality.

People everywhere seem intent on making happiness the objective of their lives instead of trying to do some good for others. Churches are losing their appeal to the rising generations. Debilitating French Existentialism took over our universities half a century ago, producing cynical and narcissistic young adults. The largest religious community is now those who say they are no longer religious but are on an individual spiritual quest. That trend is resulting in a society characterized by a pooling of mutual ignorance and gross dumbness. We live in an era in which life is incredibly challenging for the majority of societies that are trying to make sense and to do the right thing. Either Micah's metaphor is for us or we are lost.

So does it have any meaning for our time? Will it address the scattered compulsivity that is on the rise everywhere? Will it resolve the social narcissism, on the one hand, and the neurotic sense of guilt troubling so many, on the other? Can that metaphor undercut the hostile independence pervading our world and the greedy isolation that is driving it? Will Micah's metaphor do anything to shift the ground from an almost universal preoccupation with immediate gratification to a sense of durable character that grows from pain and is seasoned by the struggle for decency? What will it do for the generations that have developed with a vacuous lack of interpersonal skills, idealism, and aesthetic dignity? Will it have any influence in making gentlemen and ladies out of people anywhere?

The social revolution of the 1960s and 70s introduced an intense strain in human societies nearly everywhere in the world. Some significant constructive initiatives came from that, such as the civil rights movement, the rise of women's rights and the rights of students. However, the value system hatched in that revolution produced what Christopher Lasch called "the culture of narcissism." However, that revolution was a reaction to a flaw in the golden age of the 1940s and 50s. That was an age in which the innate human anxiety about measuring up was exaggerated. The greatest generation had created the most magnificent culture and society ever hatched upon the face of this planet and did not want that lovely world seriously disturbed. So there was a great deal of implied, though not overtly expressed, pressure for people to conform to the established norms. Following World War II there was a flood of the French philosophy of Nihilism into our university faculties. This philosophy urged the youth to resist the pressures to conform to the establishment and to cut a new path for themselves. They undertook that project with alacrity.

All of us are born scared and we learn quickly how fragile, dependent, and disempowered we are. From that knowledge we develop the coping strategy of trying to please mother, please adults, please the authorities, please others, please the government, and please the church. We develop the psychology of trying to measure up. We are never quite sure to whom and to what we need to measure up, but by the time we become cognitive at about age eight we begin to project this notion onto God. Measuring up to the expectations of everybody who can affect our lives is a large burden. We inherently want to achieve the affirmation that comes with measuring up, but we also inherently resist that pressure. Adolescence is the time when we are supposed to push against that pressure and develop our own independent identity, mindset, and course of life. It is the time for individuation and maturation.

The 1960s revolution brought in a new world order of resistance to tradition, denigration of the established values, and arrogant adolescent narcissism. Consequently it produced a society lacking a sense of history, lacking a courageous devotion to idealism, lacking an urgent investment in wholesome values, and pervaded with a psychology of manipulation and exploitation. All that revolution was self-defeating! The world is now paying the price for that misdirected individualism.

The compulsive need to measure up to parental expectations, society's demands, vocational demands, corporate conformity, the church's traditions, and divine requirements produced a loss of motivation in many folks. They decided to get off the train of life, so to speak. They created a new train of personal ambition and inventive new social patterns. Some were constructive and many were dead end streets. "Doing my own thing" deteriorated into, "If it feels good, do it." Standards of decorum which had been esteemed for centuries flew out the window for many folks, and the measures for self-certification and social affirmation were confused or lost.

The tragedy in all of that did not lie in the innovative experimentation of that social revolution. Humans in every generation have been amazing in their creative ambition for working through and moving beyond the world of their forefathers and mothers. The misfortune that was wreaked upon the world-society lay in the fact that measuring up was never the issue. Though we are born with the feeling that we are coming from behind and need to work hard to measure up, achieving that objective has never been the issue except in very superficial, social ways.

Those who love us love us as we are, not as we will be someday, not as we should be, but as we are—where we are in our pilgrimage at any given moment. God loves all of us and that message has been made adequately clear so that no one needs to be ignorant of it. So God cherishes us just as we are and where we are in our pilgrimage. God holds out before us the invitation to become what we can become, if we want to. In any case God's uncalculating and unconditional grace to all of us implies that God is delighted with exactly where we are at this moment in our life journey. God does not want us anywhere else than where we are. Are you an alcoholic, abuser, drug addict, thieving corporate executive, or some other kind of wretched sinner? God thinks you are a saint on the way to full-scale healing. God is glad for where you are on that continuum right now. So you are free to be yourself until you get sick of it for your own reasons and decide to take the next step in your pilgrimage toward being what you can become.

Measuring up is not the issue. Nor is our guilt and perfidy the issue. Nor is our inadequacy the issue. Nor is our failure the issue. Nor is our sin the issue. The only issue is God's radical and unconditional grace and forgiveness for every one of us exactly where we are right now. God has removed from the equation of our relationship with God every smidgeon of fear, guilt, or shame. We cannot avoid or lose God's forgiveness. God forgives us whether we like it or not.

God wants to free us completely so that when we decide to take the next step in our maturing and healing pilgrimage, we are free to choose that move. I have a patient who spends a double session in my clinic each week bitching and moaning about how much she wants to be free of her marriage and totally free to be herself. She is menopausal and most of her pathology derives from that, as well as her impression that she needs to run away from her life as she now has it. I have listened to her anguish now for four months and have tried to hold up a mirror of reality to help her see with what she is really dealing. Typically, she will not face the issue of menopause and get the estrogen supplement she needs. Her husband loves her dearly and is a fine gentleman who has cared for her beyond measure throughout their marriage. He has finally said to her, "Because I love you I will let you go to pursue whatever it is you need or whatever will make your life meaningful." So now I tell her each time, "You have told your story thoroughly. It is clear what is real and what is larger than life in it. However, now you are free to make the choice you need to make. You have stated your case, poured out your heartache, and declared your objectives. You can move beyond the anguish now and make the move. No one is holding you back. You are free." Of course, she does not take that step. She is getting too much meaning out of bitching and moaning and abusing her family, husband, daughter and almost anyone else around. That is the nature of the psychotic pathology menopause can sometimes bring.

God has declared unconditional forgiveness and freedom to us so that we are free from all constraints to choose our life journey. Some of us would rather persist in our neuroticisms and resistance to imagined pressure, than exercise our freedom. A large percentage of the human race would rather just bitch and moan. God invites us to freedom and joy. The issue is not our measuring up to God's standards. The issue is not our short-falls. The issue is God's unconditional and universal grace for us. "He has cast all our sins into the depths of the sea"; "For by grace we are saved, through faith, and that not of ourselves. It is a gift of God. It is not from measuring up, lest any one of us should boast that we made it into God's favor on our own merit" (Eph 2:8–9).

The reason to be a Christian is not to escape divine or human threat or pressure. The only reason to be a Christian is because it is more fun to enjoy a lifetime of living in the sunshine of knowing God guarantees that you are beloved of God in spite of your character and behavior. I think anybody who really gets that message in its radical sense always says spontaneously, "Then I want to be God's kind of person." Christianity is not an obligation to be labored at or a command to be obeyed, but an opportunity to be seized and celebrated. It is an opportunity to live in the relief and freedom of God's universal forgiving grace. God only wants us psychologically and spiritually healthy and joyful. The more we are motivated by fear, the sicker we get psychologically and spiritually. The more we live in gratitude for God's amazing gift of grace, the healthier we get psycho-spiritually.

So it should be clear by now that I must ask you if you believe that idea. Most of you will say, "Of course, I believe that. I believe in God's gift of grace." However, let me ask the question rather pointedly. Do you believe that the secret adultery that you committed, God has forgiven and forgotten altogether? Do you believe God wants you completely free of the fear, guilt, and shame of it? Do you believe that God wants you free to grow in your sense of God's grace, and to mature in Christian character? Do you believe that your adultery does not need to be eating out your heart anymore? Do you believe that it is between you and God and you may leave it there and it needs to go no further? Perhaps you fantasized it or wished you had accomplished it skillfully, but never dared. Do you believe God has forgiven you completely of whatever burden troubles your soul?

Do you believe that the parenting error that you made, God has forgiven and forgotten? Do you believe that all the wreckage it created in the life of your child, God forgave and will, like the hound of heaven, pursue that child down all his or her days and years with divine grace until God brings that child home to healing and the joy of forgiveness and unconditional acceptance? Do you believe that?

Do you believe that God has forgiven and forgotten all the ways you have betrayed someone else or your own self? Do you believe God forgives everyday your undervaluing yourself, underselling yourself, and under-asserting yourself, thus short-changing God and yourself on who you could be or become in God's world? These questions bring the matter down to pragmatic reality, of course, but that is where grace works and love heals. The Christian Way is not an abstract philosophy or a great idea one sees through rose colored glasses. It is not for arm's length use by spectators. It operates down in the mud and crap of our lives, turning it into fertilizers to make the flowers of joy grow in us. We grow from our pain. We can only be saved if we are sinners.

That is why it is so much more fun to be a Christian. Why live through all the craziness of your own adolescence in fear, guilt, and shame? Why bring up your children through precarious infancy and childhood and all the perturbations of their struggle to mature, without the assurance that God is in it with them and you, endeavoring to find the way to avert the suffering or turn it to their profit and growth? Why face life's complex responsibilities without the confidence derived from a sure sense of God's presence and grace to you? Why wrestle with the pain of your own morality and mortality without knowing the total and final solution of God's love and grace for you?

God does not love us because of the quality of our characters and behavior, even if they are stellar and pristine. God loves us and guarantees radical, unconditional, and universal grace to us because of the quality of God's character and God's characteristic behavior. God's essence is the flow of grace in the Stream of the Divine Spirit in the world. God cannot do otherwise. God cannot help God's self but to embrace us all in God's redeeming and healing grace. If God did otherwise God would not be God!

Amen. So let it Be!

SERMON TWO

Love Has Good Manners
—1 Corinthians 13:4–6

> Love has good manners . . . and is glad with all good folks when truth prevails.
> —J.B. Phillips

When I was a child I lived in a Dutch-German ghetto in the woods of northern Michigan. It was a primitive community in the decades of the Great Depression and World War II. Nonetheless, it was an idealistic community. We were materially poor but spiritually rich. Our world was controlled by a few simple principles and a lot of Dutch proverbs. We believed that there was a place for everything and everything ought to be in its place. A job worth doing was worth doing well. It was clear that the overriding principle of life was our God-given duty to leave the world a better place than we found it.

In contrast to that set of values and ideals, our American society today frequently imposes upon us a far different experience. I was sitting in a restaurant recently, waiting for the waitress to bring my breakfast, when a sudden loud noise at the entrance door drew my attention to a nineteen-year-old fellow who was slamming his way in. He let the door swing back behind him, hitting his young girlfriend squarely in the face, knocking her to the floor. He never noticed as he made his ill-mannered way to a table. She picked herself up and came laughing to him as though this entire drama was very normal behavior.

About that time the waitress appeared at my table with a plate of food which she threw down in such a way that it slid neatly over in front of me. She said, "There you go!" I said, "Where am I going? I just got here. I thought I was going to have breakfast." She could not figure out what I meant. When I paid my bill the hostess silently grabbed the money, rudely threw my change on the counter, rather than putting it into my outstretched hand, and turned on her heel.

I had to go from there to a hardware store. The owner is a friend of mine and a nice guy. He hires high school students from across the street to work in his store. To give more of them work he has a program of posting one at each door to welcome customers. I noticed a gorgeous young woman standing there to greet me. As I opened the door she said to me gruffly, "What do you want?" I guess she meant that she would be willing to direct me to the place in the store where I could get what I was after. However, I was stunned. I thought, "With friends like that, who needs enemies?"

When I returned to my office I wanted to call a friend in Ann Arbor but could not find his number. I called information and said, "I wish to have the number of Grant Schafer in Ann Arbor. His name is spelled S C H A F E R." After a long silence the operator said, "There is no Grant Schafer in Ann Arbor." I said, "Yesterday I called you for his number and you gave it to me immediately. I am sorry that I have misplaced it again." After a longer pause she said, "There is no Grant Schafer in Ann Arbor." I said, "Yes there is. I visited him there last week." She said, "No!" I said, "Yes!" She said, "How do you spell it?" I said "Schafer." She said, "There is no S H A F E R in Ann Arbor." I said, "Schafer." The exchange continued in this fashion for a number of further sequences when she said, "There is a Grant S C H A F E R in Ann Arbor." I said, "That is it!" She said, "Why didn't you tell me it was spelled funny?"

That afternoon I had to fly to Los Angeles. My flight was delayed and the gate was changed. As I leaned against a pillar, patiently waiting for the desk agent to call the flight, a very elderly couple came up, obviously confused by all the changes. An attractive young woman, who looked about thirty years of age, was working the desk. She graciously cared for the elderly couple. She explained the changes in the flight situation, informed them of where their correct gate was, ordered an electric cart, and got them on their way comfortably and happily. After watching this for about fifteen minutes, I walked up to her and said, "You must be over forty." She said, "Well, yes I am, but why do you say so?" I said, "You have good manners. I watched you care for that distressed elderly couple. I noticed that you are decent and kind." She said, "I know what you mean!"

Love has good manners. People trivialize love. Love is not merely a personal relationship. It is not merely an interpersonal relationship. It is not merely sexual communion. Those may be symptoms or indicators of love but they are not love.

Love is a matter of character. It is a characterological style, a mode of carrying oneself, a way of life. It is an outlook on living caringly and with good manners, decently and idealistically. It is the desire to carry oneself with dignity and sensitivity toward oneself and others. Love is a model for living one's life so as to enhance the well-being of others and society.

Love is not just sentimental feeling, fake sweetness and light, mere niceness, or romantic excitement. About twenty-five years ago Dorothy Tennov wrote a book entitled *Love and Limerence*, in which she clarifies the difference between love, on the one hand, and that intense electrical experience we feel when we say that we are *in love*, on the other. Her thesis was confirmed by empirical research reported in an article in *Time Magazine* entitled "The Chemistry of Love." When we experience that chemistry we call *falling in love* our bodies produce four amphetamine-like chemicals which incite an addictive kind of reaction. This lasts from four months to four years. Then it draws down and two other chemicals replace those four. Those two produce a feeling of enduring care and sustained cherishing enjoyment.

Today love is identified with sexual limerence and is not seen as important in any other circumstances. We live in a culture which is grounded out at the crotch. Such a culture can seldom get beyond the crotch to a real bonding connection of heart and the head. The electricity at the crotch is just too intense. Love is not mere limerence. Love is tough stuff, seeking the well-being of other persons or society. It does not offer what they want but what they need. Love is surgical. It is willing to turn a person inside out and upside down if that is what it takes to do them the good they need, even if they themselves do not recognize that. Family interventions with drug addicts or alcoholics are that kind of tough love.

Love Has Good Manners

This is a difficult idea to work out in our society today. In my experience as a pastor and clinical therapist as many as 40 percent of human beings in any society are mild, moderate, or severe borderline psychotics. Most of the severe ones are in hospitals or prisons. Borderlines are unable to project themselves into other people's feeling worlds or get a decent objective view of themselves. Thus they are destructively narcissistic. They cannot love. They cannot have good manners, since they are always somewhat situation-inappropriate and do not notice that they are self-preoccupied, narcissistic, and manipulative.

The good manners of love empower us to a way of life, a style of self, as gentlemen and ladies even in hellish conditions. It is a mode of idealism and dignity. Borderlines are not capable of such character. Of course, all is not lost in the Western World. Eating lunch at the Marriott some days ago I noted a very pregnant mother enter the restaurant followed by her ten year old son who was attractively dressed. He took his mother by the hand, led her to a fine table with a white table cloth, and seated her in her chair like an elegant butler. He has the good manners of real love.

You may remember the film, *The Bridge on the River Kwai,* the source of the catchy Colonel Bogie March. If you saw that film you remember it as the story of the British Forces captured by the Japanese army at Singapore in World War II. They were abused and forced into slave labor. They remained there until the last year of the war. Then they were sent on a Death March as the Japanese Forces retreated before the aggressive Allied onslaught.

You will remember that at the end of every day those British soldiers stood retreat. Their commander called them into military formation and inspected them vigorously. Then he marched them off to the mess hall where they conducted themselves as if at a formal military dinner. Their uniforms were in shreds, rotting off their shrunken bodies. The food was horrid and meager, but the Colonel demanded that they conduct themselves as gentlemen even in their extremity. There were those who saw this ritual as the arrogance of power, the joke of abusive leadership, or a ridiculous charade of military excess. Nothing was further from the truth. It was an act of love.

Colonel Bogie knew that if he could keep the internal spiritual dignity and personal discipline of his men alive, he could keep them alive. He understood that love is idealism, dignity, and politeness as an aesthetic social style. That is a love of persons and society, enhancing the commonweal. Preservation of sensitivity to beauty, kindness, and congeniality as a way of life is an act of love to the whole community. It is a way of relating to the universe with that sturdy goodness with which God relates to it. It reflects God's sense of beauty and our own. By it we enhance the total quality of things, pursuing a wholesome social order.

The former chaplain to Princeton University Chapel, The Rev. Dr. Ernest Gordon, was one of those Brits at Singapore. His book, *Through the Valley of the Quai*, sets forth graphically that those men survived the Death March who cared for the needs of others instead of being preoccupied with their own pain. Those who were not other-oriented did not live through it. Their own selfishness and narcissism produced hopelessness. The hopelessness made them feel helpless. The helplessness eventually got them.

My grandfather said that it takes three generations of wholesome people to create a great and refined character: the grandparents must will it, the parents must work it, and then the child can become it. That sounds right to me. I have seen in history that it takes five hundred years to build a civilized society and only one generation to burn it down and revert to barbarism. The rising generation of the 1960s and 70s in America tried to burn down the very best achievement humans had ever accomplished on the face of this planet. I did not say "perfect." I said the best until then. We are still suffering today and in detail from the narcissistic backwash of that counterproductive phase of adolescent craziness. It was a very near thing for our culture. We may never get over its consequences. The flower children sang, "Make love, not war" while they drugged themselves into oblivion and developed into permanent fascistically self-centered immaturity. They thought love meant being joined at the crotch.

Christianity is about a way of love that is a constructive way of life. It is a personal style of decency. Elegant language is not prissiness, it is good taste. Opening a door for a woman is not condescending devaluation, it is esteem. Dignity in public and private is not prudishness, it is honor. Christianity is about humane values, humane idealism, and the good manners of genuine love.

Christianity has a flawed history but what is notable is that on the whole it civilizes persons and communities, *because* love has good manners. Where Christianity has deviated from that it has been mean and obscene, abusive, violent, and destructive. Thomas Cahill's book, *How the Irish Saved Civilization* and Lord Kenneth Clark's series, *Civilisation* make the point that while the world was diving into the Dark Ages after the fall of the Roman Empire, it was the dignity and idealism preserved in the Irish monasteries that saved Christianity "by the skin of its teeth." Christian love has the good manners that save life, society, and civilization.

That is the reason I am still for the church, despite all its deficits. It is the only institution left in our society which at least intends to stand for truth, righteousness, grace, love, decency, justice, kindness, and gentility. Christianity is about God's love and ours and such love has good manners.

Amen. So let it Be!

SERMON THREE

God and Beauty
—Genesis 1:1, 1:31; Psalm 19:1–4

> God saw all that God had made and God said, "It is *very good*!"
> — GENESIS 1:31A

THE MOST ACCURATE AND important thing that you can ever say about God is that God is an artist. The first thing that God says in the Bible is, "Let there be light"; and so there was light. And the very second thing God says in the Bible is, *It is very good. It is beautiful!* (Gen. 1:31b) Rembrandt became the most important painter of the Dutch Golden Age of art because of how much he appreciated the importance of light. The thing that made his paintings stand out as distinctive in all the history of art was the way in which he used light. Rembrandt discovered that if you use light just right, with a minimum of everything else and the right touch of light, you can say things with a painting that are not even literally in the picture. Rembrandt understood that the way light is employed can tell the psychological story of how the people in the picture were feeling. He perceived that light is what gives everything meaning.

God and Beauty

Ever since Rembrandt, no one has been able to create great art without tending to the unique function of light. Van Gogh used light differently. You have seen his painting, *Starry Night*, in which even the title reveals how importantly he thought art depended upon what you did with light. He painted many canvases. In all of them what makes Van Gogh distinctive is the way he used thick swirls of paint to emphasize the function of light and shadow. He caused the light to fall on the canvas in special ways by the aggressive waves and swatches of heavy paint, applied with a knife, or his thumb, or a heavy brush. Light is everything in art. My daughter is a professional artist. You should see what she does with trees and skies and seascapes just by the presentations of light.

God said, "Let there be light!" By that word God wrote the divine signature on the universe. God is the greatest artist in history, and God saw the light, and in that light God saw everything else that was created (Gen 1:31) and God said, *It is really very good, immensely beautiful!* Can you hear the tremor in God's voice? Somewhere between crying for joy and laughing for joy, God said, *Wow! This is really magnificent!*

It is clear from the first chapter of Genesis and from most of the rest of the Bible that for God the chief issue is beauty. That is why I wanted to talk to you this morning about God and beauty. The first reason why I believe in God is the mindful nature of the evolving universes and the life in them. The second reason why I believe in God is that everything in God's creation always moves irrepressibly toward beauty. Everything in the whole universe always moves toward growth, development, unfolding, blossoming, and fruitfulness—inevitably moving toward beauty. Gordon Bok, the poet and musician thought that all things are always *turning toward the morning*.

Three weeks ago I looked out my office window and there I saw, poking up through the wood chips, about an inch of a green spear. I asked Mary Jo, "What is that thing out there?" It could have been the chives she planted, or a tulip, a jonquil, a daffodil, or a crocus. It could have been some mysterious thing from an alien movie. She said, "We will have to wait to see what it becomes, but we know it will be beautiful." Now, three weeks later we know. It is a blooming crocus. It has moved from a tiny spear to a blossoming flower, just like God designed it to become. It's, indeed, a funny hocus-pocus to have a purple crocus poke us into spring.

God is into beauty more than anything else and more than any of us! What I want to say loudly and clearly this morning is that God's whole purpose in history is beauty. Now, I know that sounds like a radical sort of reductionism but think about it. I think that the only thing that God stakes God's life on, so to speak, the only thing God would fall on a sword over, is beauty. It seems clear to me that if you read the Bible carefully, you will notice that throughout there is God's hope for and celebration of *beauty*—in persons and things. What gets your attention all the time throughout that first chapter of Genesis is the fact that God keeps on saying, *Wow! Its great! It is really good. This stuff I have made is really beautiful!*

That is, God celebrates all the beauty. I think that is true of everything God is up to. God is mainly into beauty! Thomas Aquinas would want to make the argument that what God is mainly into is truth: rational, logical, empirical, imperative truth. I do not think God is very hung up on whether we end up getting all the dogmas of Christian doctrine down with exact precision. After all, why would God have gone to all the cost and trouble of radical, unconditional, and universal grace if the main issue were our getting everything just right? It bothers me that some people think that God forgives all sins except theological mistakes. How absurd. That is not God's focus.

I want to make the case that truth is important to God only as a subsidiary category to beauty. When you create beauty you need to create authenticity. Rembrandt cannot use a false or fake manipulation of light and expect that to be great art. That would be ugliness, not beauty. If the light shines on the left cheek of the woman praying over her meager meal, while in fact the light is coming in through the window on the opposite side of the room, it would be more than a *faux pas*. That would be failed art! It would not reflect the reality required by a great painting. It would be inauthentic, not true to life. Beauty implies authenticity. It implies truth! Truth is important to God, I am sure, but it is a subcategory to beauty in God's perspective. It may even be an accidental corollary of beauty.

I think you have to say the same of morality. It is interesting that in the whole human race, whether you are a believer or a secularist who does not take God seriously, morality is always the big deal. Why do we make so much of morality? Why are we so strung out about morality? Well, I suppose it is to keep the world safe and orderly; to keep marriages safe and orderly; to compel the Enron executives to steal a little less; to urge people to respect their contracts and commitments a little more. I think God is interested in that. I think God is interested in an orderly moral society.

But I suspect that the reason God is for morality lies in the fact that the lack of it is so unacceptably ugly. I believe God is interested in morality

God and Beauty

because it is a function of beauty. Remember that God is completely committed to easily forgiving immorality: all of it, for everybody, throughout all the world. God arbitrarily removes all fear, guilt, and shame from our relationship with God, so that our psycho-spiritual energies are completely available for our growth, development, blossoming, and bearing the fruit of maturity and wholesomeness. God has made it clear that God can forgive the worst kind of stuff at the drop of a hat, so to speak. God has insisted upon a radical investment of grace everywhere in this world, so you can see that God is not primarily hung up on morality.

We play the game of being preoccupied with the restrictions of morality because we do not want to honor the imperatives of beauty, and we like jacking each other around with moral manipulation and controls. Because we are lazy or sick or greedy or screwed up in some way or another, we play around the edges of morality, which reflects the fact that we do not take beauty seriously enough—beautiful life, beautiful world. The world of the Enron executives and the bank presidents and the Wall Street manipulators that destroyed our economy is not a beautiful world. It is an ugly world.

The world created by the fact that in America 52 percent of all marriages end in divorce is an ugly world. Of course some of them should end in divorce, sooner and not later. Indeed they should never have been contracted. The world would be a lot uglier if many marriages had not ended in divorce. God is against it for the ugliness of it. It defiles, undermines, and undercuts the beauty of a covenanted society, the beauty in the security of a cherishing relationship. God is against it because it creates ugliness instead of a beautiful world. So, I think God is for truth and God is for morality because the lack of it is downright ugly.

You can say the same for honor. I am certain God wants honorable people. We admire honorable people because we discern inherently, without being taught it, that there is something beautiful about a man of honor and about an honorable woman. I remember that as elementary students we held George Washington up as a paragon of Americanism, without picking at his obvious humanness. He was an honorable man. George Washington's remarkable characteristics tell us what kind of honorable person he was. We inherently sense that the fact that he stands there at the beginning and, as the father of our country, imbues our country with some remarkable honor. People like that created and accrued a reservoir of ethical capital for our country. We ought to be careful not to waste or erode it away.

By Grace Alone

Why is that imperative so important to us? Because honorable people stand for a beautiful world! America is a more beautiful place, indeed, the last great hope of the world, because honorable men and women adorn the stages of our history. They were beautiful and they make us beautiful by their honor. Of course they were human and hence flawed. No age of history was perfect or ideal. However, I grew up in a time when we were schooled in a larger-than-life appreciation of Washington, James Madison, John Adams, Thomas Jefferson, Alexander Hamilton, Abraham Lincoln, and Ulysses S. Grant. I noticed that when my children went to school the teachers were attempting to be much more realistic about the humanness of those folks. They seemed to me to be working overtime devaluing those heroic figures. The issue at stake for every generation has to do with the degree to which we appreciate that those great figures who stood for honor, truth, and morality gave to our country a quality of beauty.

They may not have been physically beautiful. Grant drank so much alcohol, despite his great success as a general, that Lincoln said he would like to find out what Grant drank so he could send a barrel of it to each of his generals. Lincoln was so physically unattractive that a little girl had the temerity to tell him to grow a beard to cover up his face. He was once accused of being two-faced, to which he replied, "If I were two-faced, would I be wearing this one?" It was their beauty of character that counted. Grant had the heroic wisdom to advance the sacred cause of freedom and democracy and bring a terrible war to a quick end. Lincoln negotiated the shoals and rapids of the worst time in American history with towering wisdom and abiding faith in the guiding presence of the Divine Spirit.

If you take that idealism away from children, you take away a sense of the beauty of this country. Maybe that is why we get what we have today, an age when citizens do not seem ready to stand up for the honor, truth, and beauty of this country like I seem to remember we used to do. I think it comes down to the issue that God makes very plain in the Bible: beauty always depends upon a covenanted relationship, that is, a sense of mutuality that creates a beautiful world by insuring all of us that we are secure in a connectedness in which we cherish each other and can count on that cherishing from others. We are all called to stand for the honor, moral integrity, and the authenticity or truth in each other. That used to work in America. That is what creates a beautiful world, and I think that is what answers to God's intent and ambition for God's world.

God and Beauty

Any community that lives for cultivating a culture of the Divine Spirit is going to be focused upon and live out the pursuit of that beauty which God intends in the world. There is an interesting passage in one of the later prophets. It declares that when the kingdom of God comes fully in this world, "Holiness unto the Lord" will be written on the temple vessels used for carrying away the contents of the intestines of the sacrificed animals. On the bridles of the horses shall be written, "Holiness unto the Lord" (Zech 14:20–21a). Why would the prophet have picked those two rather odd items? You know how filthy with green froth the bridles of horses can become after they have worked hard or run a race. You can imagine the filth in those vessels of the temple. Yet they shall be inscribed as holy unto the Lord.

Holiness does not mean purity. Holiness means perfection in a special sense, namely, that the vessels and bridles, or God's people, are serving the purpose for which they have been called and set aside. When the world is embellished and renewed the way God intends to save and heal it everything and everyone will be answering well to those roles and styles for which we are called and set aside by God. We will all be constructive parts of God's renewed world. *Everything* will be holy unto the Lord. You and I are beautiful and holy in the sight of God when we are answering to what we are called for and what we are dedicated to in God's economy. Those vessels and bridles were doing the job they were called to do. How can we legitimately write the slogan on the gates of our inner cities, "Holiness unto the Lord" ? We should figure that out. It seems like an important job. God is into beauty reflected in holiness to the Lord.

Yesterday I got a call from a friend that you might call a brother. Dan Greenberg has no brother so he adopted me as his brother thirty years ago. We taught together in the same department at Oakland for many years. He called me to say that his lovely wife Roz, my dear friend, is dying. She had cancer years ago and it has now returned with a vengeance. She is in her last weeks. So I went to see her at the nursing home. Dan and Roz and their family are Jewish believers. I talked with her about the consolations that one finds in the Hebrew Bible, the Old Testament.

I asked her if she liked Psalm 23. She was glad to talk about its importance for a time like this and we recited it together in English and in Hebrew. She was particularly touched, of course, as was I, when we reached the fourth verse, "Even though I walk through the valley of the shadow of death, I will fear no evil!" That is where she was right then. I asked her what she would like me to read after that. She said she wanted to hear again the words of Psalm 19:1–4. Why did she want to read that? She said it was because she wanted to be reminded of the beauty of God. "The heavens declare the glory of God, and the sky shows forth God's handiwork." So we recited that together and prayed.

It was a great consolation to her to think of God as the God of beauty, as her body, which had been really beautiful, was wasting away. When you think about it, the thing that gives us deep consolation is not the fact that God is the God of truth or morality or carefully worked-out theological doctrines and ethics. I am sure God is for those things, though probably not for the inordinate amount of time humans have wasted on them. What gives me consolation in life, however, is not that God is a God of honor, truth, or morality but that all of these things are important because they represent those essences of God that let us know who God really is, the great artist of the universe. God is the great orchestrator of the symphony of grace! God guarantees against all odds, even the odds of death, that nothing will ever be able to destroy the beauty of the human spirit embraced by God's grace. All of us need that grace every day, and the further we go along the road, the closer we are to needing it desperately.

The great English poet, John Keats, said magnificently and conclusively, "Beauty is truth, and truth beauty. That is all you know in life and all you need to know."

Amen. So let it Be!

SERMON FOUR

He Who Has the Most Toys Wins

—Psalm 107:8–9; Luke 12:13–21

THE VALUE OF A person's life is not measured by material possessions.

I have a neighbor who has two dogs, two boats, two snowmobiles, two skidoos, two four wheelers, an old Jaguar, a new BMW, two golf carts, and an electric runabout that he drives around the subdivision. Of course, he also has two trailers to truck these things around in, so his garage is too full to make room for his cars. Yesterday he came over to borrow my lawn mower. I asked him why, with all the machinery he has, he does not have a lawn mower. He said he has a lawn mower but it is broken and he cannot afford to repair it just now. He is thirty-four years old and he believes that whoever has the most toys when he dies wins.

It reminded me of the Prodigal Son in Jesus' parable. He wanted it all now! I mentioned the fellow in our scripture for today who said to Jesus, "Master, make my brother divide with me the inheritance due me" (Lu 12:13–21). Jesus was impatient with him and asked why he thought Jesus was a judge and an arbitrator for him. Of course, the problem Jesus had with him and with the Prodigal was not that they desired something that was not due them. In both cases these fellows wanted what was rightfully theirs. They were justly seeking their own rightful possessions. So the problem was not that they desired something they had no right to desire.

Nor was the problem the matter of desire or appetite and seeking one's rights in itself. If I were a Buddhist priest instead of a Christian priest, I would be tempted to say that the reason Jesus was impatient with the man in our text was that desire, in itself, is the source of all our trouble. Buddhism teaches that desire produces unfulfilled longings. Those longings produce suffering and pain. That ruins life by making us greedy and prompting us to think we can feel better with more fulfillment of our desires. Therefore, Buddhism thinks that material things are evil objects of our destructive desires. So life's main problems will be solved by eliminating desire in the first place and withdrawing from this material world into the world of the spirit.

But Jesus was not a Buddhist and that is not what he had in mind here. Notice that in Jesus' parable of the Prodigal Son (Luke 15:11–32), the father, who represents God, does not reprimand the son for his desire to have his inheritance. The father goes along quietly with the son's request and is silent throughout the entire parable until he welcomes the son home with open arms.

The problem in both of these cases is neither desire for something that should not be desired, nor the evil of desire in itself. The problem Jesus has with the fellow asking for Jesus' help seems to be something deeper. Jesus has a problem with the common notion that the meaning of *things* that will satisfy a person lies in the possession of the things in themselves. The Prodigal Son says he wants to have his stuff so he can go out and cut his own swath in life, so to speak. The father silently waits for the son to discover that he will probably not find the meaning of his life in that freedom and power, even though there is nothing inherently wrong with taking charge of one's own destiny.

The man in our text makes Jesus uncomfortable because Jesus is impatient with this fellow's assumption, namely, that the meaning of his life will be found in his acquisition of the things he is due. Jesus closes the paragraph by declaring, "A man's life does not consist in the abundance of the things he possesses" (Luke 12:15b). It is not true that he who has the most toys when he dies wins.

So Luke wisely follows this incident with the parable of the successful farmer who farmed so wisely that he had to build larger barns (Luke 12:16–21), but just then he dropped dead! I am sure that in the last two thousand years, two thousand sermons on this parable have claimed that the parable is about the evil of riches. Let me apprise you of the fact that the parable is not about that. Jesus was not against riches or rich people. He hung out with them whenever he was not hanging out with whores and thieves. Think of Zacchaeus, Joseph of Arimathea, Simon the Pharisee, the three sons of Zebedee, and many other rich guys. Jesus liked them and he especially liked eating with them at the luxurious banquets in their palatial homes. Jesus had a good taste for fine food and plenty of good wine. It was not accidental that his main reputation was that he was an enormous eater and lusty drinker, and a friend of thieving tax collectors and women of the street.

It is clear that the problem with the successful farmer was not that he was a very good farmer, nor that he produced a super-abundance of crops, nor that he decided to store the excess wisely and well. His problem was not that he was a good planner and therefore also a richly successful farmer. After all, God intends all of us to be millionaires. God made us for the Garden of Eden, the ultimate in luxury and abundance. God intends us all to be richly blessed, wise, and luxuriant. The farmer's problem was not that he was rich, nor that he decided to retire early. The problem of the farmer was that he died that night—and it caught him unawares.

Now, let us not be too hard on this guy. I am over eighty. I might drop dead tonight and if I do I can assure you it will catch me unawares because I am not planning on it. I am not quite like Sam Goldwyn when he was dying of cancer. His friend asked him how he was doing and Sam said, "If I dropped dead today I would be the happiest man alive." I am not at that point, and neither was the rich farmer. His problem was not that he was rich, luxuriant, and retiring. His problem was that he did not plan on his mortality. He was busy living his life wisely in the midst of his things but he had not gotten around to living his life before the face of God and under pressure of eternity.

This is not a passage of scripture about the sinfulness of riches. There are no such scriptures in the whole Bible. This is a scripture about having a good will, in both senses of that word. Jesus asks, "Whose shall these things be?" It is not true that he who has the most toys when he dies wins. Being rich is God's intent for us, but not at the expense of others nor in a life that tries to find its meaning in living amidst one's abundance of things rather than living consciously before the face of God. If you spend more time polishing your boat than reading your Bible, you may have things somewhat out of proportion. You may want to reconsider that. Think about it.

By Grace Alone

A brilliant professor, Christopher Lasch, wrote *The Culture of Narcissism*. He was analyzing the American culture and society of the late twentieth century. I do not know whether our culture is a narcissistic culture or whether it is instead just a society of obsessive-compulsive people desperate to fill its spiritual hunger for meaning with a world full of material things. Perhaps it is a lunge for security through having enough objects of gratification that we can quiet the longing of our souls for God and heaven, or just for some earthly peace and tranquility. How many things does that take? When is enough *enough*? Ever? "A man's life does not consist in the abundance of the things he possesses." Nor does a woman's!

Things are really good in and of themselves and they are good to have, but not at the expense of others and not as the source and focus of the meaning of life. I would not give up my refrigerator and go back to trying to preserve milk and butter by setting them down in the basement next to the cold water tank, as we did when I was a child. Can you imagine the Garden of Eden without free bananas? But life was just as meaningful in the deprivation of the 1930s as it is in 2012. My ministry is a quest for deep inner spirituality. That is what I find meaningful.

I am sure that when Jesus responded to the man in our text and told the parable of the rich farmer, he heard ringing in the back of his head the words of Psalm 107:8–9, "Oh that the people of God would praise God for God's goodness, and for God's wonderful works for humankind, for *God satisfies the longing soul, filling the hungering spirit with *divine* goodness.*" He who has the most toys does not win because of them. That is not the way things are wired. The world is two-dimensional: material and spiritual. The former without the latter tends to be empty.

What about you? Do you spend more time polishing your boat, or reading your Bible?

Amen. So let it Be!

SERMON FIVE

Mercy and Not Sacrifice: A Stewardship Sermon
—Matthew 9:1–13

I desire mercy and not sacrifice.
I came not to call the righteous but sinners.

— Matthew 9:13a

A PASTOR WENT TO a remote island to vacation with his son. While he was there over a weekend the local church, small and needy, discovered him and asked if he would conduct the service on Sunday. He said that he would be delighted. He arrived early for the 10:00 service. He got there before anyone else. The door was unlocked, he went in, acquainted himself with the setting of worship, tried to get the feel of the pulpit and the chancel area, and then noticed that next to the entrance door there was a rustic mission box. He reached into his pocket, found two quarters, and dropped them into the box.

A small congregation gathered. He provided an inspiring service and prepared to leave. The Chief Elder said, "Pastor it's our custom here that whatever is in the Mission Box after the service goes to the Pastor for the sermon." He went to the Mission Box and encouraged his son to see what they had made that morning. He found just those two quarters, so his son said to him, "Well dad, if you'd have put more in you'd have got more out." That seems to be the way it is in life.

I had a counselee on Friday—a lady from England who is suffering, unfortunately, from depression. One of the ways in which her depression manifests itself is that she has a kind of a negative view of nearly everything in the world and on Friday she had a particularly negative view about life in America. We talked about that a little while and I suggested that she sounded like she was digging herself a deeper hole in her depression and that she might consider reframing her cognitive ideas. I suggested particularly that her very negative view of the church was probably something that she could benefit from changing. She said, "Well, I have always been troubled by the fact that the church is full of hypocrites." I thought immediately of my father's response to that complaint. He always said, "Well dear, there is always room for one more." So I said that to her. She had a negative view of my saying so.

But it is the truth that in things spiritual as well as in things material, if you put more in you get more out. Personal spirituality always responds that way in my experience. It works to invest in the practice of the presence of God.

That is not only true of spirituality. I have had a number of different kinds of jobs in my life, particularly while I was working my way through school. I shoveled coal for quite a long time. Then I drove a garbage truck—one of the better jobs I had. I drove a building materials delivery truck. I was a farmer. I worked in the factory at Keeler Brass dipping Ford handles in chrome brine—probably one of the worst jobs I ever had. I was a hod carrier for brick layers. I was a soldier and I was a teacher.

Every one of those jobs was interesting to me because of a specific characteristic that I developed somewhere along the way of life. It is probably a gift from God. I was always able and motivated to find a new and more efficient way of doing what I had to do. That was true whether I was cleaning the stables of cow manure or something more sophisticated than that, like working as assistant grade foreman on road construction. The enjoyment of discovering that there are new ways to do things better, more efficiently, and more quickly is an enormous gratification. It usually only requires a little extra energy and thought. If you put more in you get more out 100 percent of the time.

Jesus said to his disciples, "God wants mercy, not sacrifice." That is an interesting statement to think about. Mercy and not sacrifice! Most of us take the approach in the Church that it is our job to sacrifice. The Church needs energy. It needs hours of our time. It needs work from us, and money. It needs an awful lot of things to continue to be what the believing community needs to be to serve the world. It is true of all aspects of life. We are very much aware of what it costs every one of us in diligent labor and devotion to make sure that the democracy of our country can survive and prosper. The more you put in the more you get out. The more diligent you are in making the decisions that need to be made for our country and for the church, the more fruitful life can be. If you put more in, you get more out.

God wants mercy and not sacrifice. I am sure that every one of you would have been surprised if I had started out my sermon by saying that God does not want sacrificial gifts from you. Or if I had started out by saying God does not need your money. That would be a risky declaration, would it not? I could have begun by saying God does not need your gifts. God can do the business of the Church without you. God will find the resources and the ways to do it. However, God is not inclined to do it without us. God prefers to do it with us. God invites us, more than God commands us, to be participants in the life and in the cost of what it takes to be a vital, healthy, and healing presence in the world. God invites spontaneous devotion.

However, God desires mercy, not sacrifice. I recently published four volumes in which one of the chapters was written by Raphael Chodos. The title of his chapter is "God Does Not Want Obedience—He Abhors It." Now it's a surprise to hear something like that. God abhors obedience. The thrust of Raphael's chapter is that God delights in our spontaneous response to God's invitation for us to be partners with God in the redemptive work in the world. But God assuredly does not want us laboring in that endeavor out of the motivation of obedience to a command. God wants us to work in God's enterprises out of the joyfulness of our delight in authentic service. In that service, the more you put in the more you get out. God does not want sacrifice. God wants mercy that springs from our gratitude for all the peace and relief God's grace affords us.

So as we approach the issue of stewardship and talk about money, time, and energy invested for the Church, we mean to raise our consciousness level about the specific material needs of the Church. In that area God wants mercy and not sacrifice. Now how do we do that? Well, we look at our world and we look at our church and we look at each other and we look at ourselves. Then we ask what would be the merciful thing to do here? What does the world need? What does the church need? What do my fellow parishioners need? What do the children of our congregation need? What do I need? That is, what works of mercy are just waiting here to be met?

What is the need out there to which we can be profoundly merciful? If we can identify *that,* then we will have no sense of burdensomeness as we go about our ministry in the Church. Even our sacrifice in the Church will not be burdensome sacrificial obedience because under the rubrics I just described it will not feel like sacrifice. It will feel like the joyful opportunity to mercifully meet the needs that arise in our assessment of what we ought to be up to together. We will have mercy. So our stewardship will not be a sacrificial burden to us. It will feel like the joy and gratification of generosity of spirit.

If it becomes a burden I fully agree with this scripture that we should not do it. If you feel that what the Church is asking of you is an obligation, and it is a burden for you, then I think that is not what you are supposed to be doing. I think that is going too far in terms of your resources. God wants mercy. God wants you and me to meet the needs out there. To meet them with a great sense of urgency and joyfulness, realizing that need is exactly what we have the ability by the grace of God to meet. So God wants mercy, not sacrifice. No burden! Give in terms of the need and your ability to service it so it will be a free and joyful act of mercy.

My uncle was a farmer in our northern Michigan community. I remember him sitting numerous afternoons in the living room of our home in deep and long conversations with my father about this issue of stewardship. His view was that the more money you put into the collection plate the more potatoes grew on your vines. He really believed that. Well, that would be a difficult one to test empirically. I am disinclined to believe it. Nonetheless, God said through his Old Testament prophet, "Try me and see if I will not open the windows of heaven for you" (Mal 3:10b). So Uncle Harm had a good word on which to base his claim.

I think Jesus' declaration that God loves mercy and not sacrifice means that we are not to give sacrificially. Do not give until it hurts. Do not give obligingly. Identify the needs for the church's ministries of mercy and then give hilariously! If you put more of yourself into it you will get more of the gratifications of the Spirit out of it.

Amen. So let it Be!

SERMON SIX

A Usable Future
—Matthew 16:13–19

On this rock I will build my church and the evil powers shall not be able to withstand it..

— MATTHEW 16:18

CREATIONISTS ARGUE AGAINST THE theory of evolution because they make the assumption that the Bible is a textbook on zoology, geology, biology, and such other scientific disciplines. It is not a textbook on anything! Bishop Usscher of the seventeenth century took it as a textbook on history and computed the age of the world on the basis of it. He concluded that God created the world in 4006 BCE, on a Tuesday morning at 10:15. He was slightly in error! The Bible is not even a textbook on theology, spirituality, or religion. It is simply not a textbook on anything.

It is a book of collected stories from which the implications of certain theological insights can be drawn. Mainly, it is an attempt to report the way in which many people over a three thousand year period perceived God's nature and behavior in their lives. This gave them some insight into how humans stand, and ought to stand, before the face of God. The stories in the Bible are all personal stories of individuals and of a community. These stories report a pattern of faith-vision and spiritual experience that they perceived to be God's story in their lives. Occasionally they were correct in their perceptions.

So the Bible is not a textbook for anything but *it is very definitely* one important thing. It is a constitution for a usable future for the believing community, the church and synagogue. In that regard, the Bible makes three things clear. First, God creates the church's and the synagogue's usable future day by day. It is not preset by some inflexible and fatalistic predestination. Thus it requires human creative thought and faithful action every day to make the quest of faith fruitful.

The church is God's action agency for the implementation of the kingdom of God on earth. In that sense, the church is an *ad hoc* institution. It exists only for that kingdom task and only for the time that task takes. It is not some transcendent, heavenly, or eternal institution. It exists to implement God's rule of love that works and grace that heals in this temporal world. As such, the church is to be an aggressive challenge to the powers of this world which demean or truncate divinely intended growth in persons, communities, and institutions.

It is clear from the text of scripture that the bastions of evil in this world will not be able to stand up against the church's God-ordained aggression. I grew up hearing this text explained in a very different way. "The gates of hell shall not prevail against the church (Matt 16:18)," was portrayed as a pathetic defensive posture on the part of the church. It seemed to me to be a fainthearted hope against hope that under the onslaughts of evil doers the church would survive; even if only a remnant, and by the skin of its teeth. That is a bad misreading of the text. The biblical message here means to say that the church is aggressively on the march. It is headed for an invasion of the bastions of evil themselves. The hellishness will not be able to resist the onslaught of the church.

Origen, a notable third century Christian theologian, said that hell itself would be emptied and the devil himself rehabilitated by the onslaught of God's aggressive message of forgiving grace. It is clear from the text that Jesus sees the powers of the hellishness in this world to be beleaguered by the forces of the kingdom of God, the reign of God's love and grace.

Secondly, the foundation of the church is on the bedrock of Peter's confession, "You are the Messiah." The church is not built upon the foundation of the man, Peter. Three verses after Peter's confession, Jesus cursed

A Usable Future

Peter, calling him a devil and a stumbling block to Jesus' mission. Mark's gospel informs us, in fact, that Jesus did not like the meaning Peter was giving to the word *Messiah* or *Christ*. Peter meant the Messiah as an earthly king on David's throne, who would throw out the Romans and reestablish Israel as an independent nation. Peter's Messiah concept was that of a political and social leader who would set right the government and society. Jesus saw himself as the Messiah, the Son of Man who came from heaven to reveal the divine mysteries of God's unconditional and universal grace to all humans. Jesus foresaw that his mission was a dangerous one that would lead to a collision with the established religious authorities. By the last years of his life he realized that his mission would result in his suffering and death.

Jesus' claim is simple. The believing community is always founded on and defined by Peter's confession, authentically interpreted. Wherever people confess Jesus as the Christ, the church already exists. Many Christians pride themselves in belonging to a confessional church. We hold to creeds and theological formulations which we cherish as our confessions of faith. Jesus made it clear that the church is founded upon Peter's specific confession. The church is God's action agency for healing, freedom, and redemption in the world. Jesus asserted that the confessional church is on the march and the forces of distraction, denigration, destruction, and degradation shall not be able to resist its conquest of the world. Love, grace, and spiritual freedom will prevail. Every one of us wishes it were victorious in our day.

Thirdly, it is clear from the Bible that nothing good is going to happen in the life of the Church unless we cause it to happen. My father frequently observed that "We are God's agents of sanctification in our own lives and in our world." He was sure that the Christian confession of Christ as Lord led to five consequences in our growth in godliness: God's election of us as God's people and leading to our vocation to live as God's people. This implies our justification by God's grace and our sanctification, that is, our maturity and increased godliness through life's experience with God. Our faith leads us ultimately to our glorification in heaven.

So the church is a community of people who live by a spiritual vision, in a process of spiritual growth, and enact in that process the kingdom of God's love and grace in this world. Thus we are the people of God engaged in the task of delivering those who are merely muttering along in meaningless spiritual lives. Our vocation is to entice them into the love, grace, and freedom of being participants and proponents of God's reign of uncalculating forgiveness of every human being.

Jesus said, "I will give you the keys of the kingdom. Whoever you bind or loose on earth shall be bound or loosed in heaven" (Matt 16:19). This does not say, "saved or condemned." It speaks of both categories of bound and loosed being in heaven. Obviously Jesus means that those to whom we are able to get across in this life the real nature of God's total forgiveness and grace shall enter heaven in full-orbed freedom and spiritual maturity. Those to whom we are unable to get that across will enter heaven spiritually pinched, constrained, and harried. They will certainly be coming from behind as they start their life eternal in God's all-embracing grace and forgiveness since it will be a brand new experience for them.

So the issue comes down to a simple question: how does one confess that Jesus is Christ or Christ is Lord? How do we articulate that truth, as the church on the march against the hellishness of this world and against the damnation and demeaning with which evil curses human lives?

We need a model in our minds and hearts. The Parish Model translates the confession into action by cultivating and serving the internal fellowship of the congregation. That model depends upon the congregation for the action of renewal and for reaching our community as individual members of a congregation. The purpose of the Parish Model is to progressively add the community to the congregation. In this model the emphasis is upon worship, education, and service to the needs of our community. Most churches are operating in terms of this Parish Model. Is that enough? Is that good enough?

An alternative is the Cathedral Model. This one is centralized in a worship service designed to attract attention and create something of a spiritual spectacle. This model anticipates that the church and its liturgies will become noteworthy and notable throughout the city as a distinctive aesthetic site and celebration. This model is centered in a spectacular cathedral edifice and focuses upon the performance of the clergy and musicians, funded by the congregation, and cultivating satellite groups in adjacent communities. The function of the satellites is to provide the ministries of education, fellowship, and charitable services to members and community inquirers. The intent of this model is to provide pastoral support to members of the congregation and to serve the interests and needs of community people where they live. The Megachurches are organized in a general way on this Cathedral Model.

This model is less geographically conscious and more operationally conscious. It expresses itself in local assemblies of service, spiritual fellowship, and community life. The Cathedral Church functions then as a place of consolation, inspiration, imagination, and invigoration, as well as an aesthetic center of beauty and celebration. The life of the church will always be as cramped or as spacious as our vision allows and creates.

The Mission Center Model envisions a parish church primarily as an agency to take the city into its hands as a garden of social service. The focus of the whole organism addresses the challenge of changing or strengthening parish life and ministry throughout our community, strengthening or changing structures of the city and its institutions, and of being the agency through which the various forces for good in the community can be united and channeled toward eliminating suffering, inequity, and injustice.

There are, of course, other models, as well, such as the Ecclesiastical Park Model, which envisions a kind of city within the city, a self-sufficient community in which worship centers, clinics, service agencies, educational institutions, and homes for the aged or indigent are all part of the church's institution, work, community, and world in a special enclave within the larger urban area.

Nothing good will happen to the church's future unless we cause it to happen. We are God's action agents to build the church and assault the hellish injustice, lack of mercy, and corrupt institutions in our world. We are the people of God for our time. It is up to us to take our confession, history, vision, and posture before the face of God, and give it a palpably applied operation in God's world—in our town. This means cultural and social salvation and redemption arising out of personal spiritual renewal. Jesus plainly said that whatever we bind or set free on earth will enter heaven pinched and twisted or enjoying the glorious freedom of the people of God. Does that not mean that what we achieve on earth has eternal consequences? Whether we get across to folks the central fact that God's grace is radical, unconditional, and universal has eternal consequences, indeed! Those who have come to realize that nobody can ever in any way fall out of God's forgiving grace, and no one, however evil, can squirm out of God's forgiving embrace, can live life joyfully free and enter eternity with advanced placement in spiritual maturity.

Amen. So let it Be!

SERMON SEVEN

As a Dying Man
—1 Corinthians 9:16–18

Woe is me if I preach not the gospel... I proclaim the gospel as free of charge.
—1 Corinthians 9:16b

Recently I had the pleasure of commissioning a friend of mine as a Second Lieutenant in the US Army. It reminded me of the fact that on June 10, 1955, I was commissioned as a Second Lieutenant, beginning a thirty-seven year military career from which I retired as a Colonel. When I received my commission as an army officer I realized that it had very special meaning. It meant that from that point on my life was not my own. My life belonged to the cause. When one puts on the uniform of a military officer or a policeman one makes a statement by that act. It is a commitment to the commission that life is not one's own any longer and never will be again. It means that if there is going to be any dying it will be me and not the noncombatant citizens of the community or country for whose well-being one is commissioned.

That sense of being commissioned, knowing that my life is no longer my own, was not a new experience for me in 1955. From age seven I knew

As a Dying Man

that I was called of God to preach the gospel, commissioned to ministry. My life would never again belong to me but to the cause, God's cause! You can see that for me my life has never really been my own.

When Paul wrote our scripture for today he expressed that same consciousness. Four phrases stand out in the scripture we read: "I proclaim the gospel. Woe is me if I do not proclaim the gospel! I am entrusted with a commission . . . I proclaim the gospel as free of charge" (1 Cor 9:16–18). From the day of my commissioning until this moment as I step into this pulpit, that word, *commissioned*, has held a weighty significance for me and I notice that it held a weighty significance for Paul. "I am entrusted with a commission to proclaim the gospel as being free of charge. Woe is me if I do not proclaim the gospel." His life was not his own. His life belonged to the cause of God and the gospel.

Paul speaks in these impassioned tones about what it meant for him to be a missionary for God. He also has this interesting side-argument going here. He says, You know, I could preach just for the fame of being a great preacher but the fact is that I preach because I am under the compulsion of a commission. I preach because my life is not my own. It belongs to God and God's cause. Moreover, it is clear from the way Paul talks about his ministry in all of his epistles and especially in 1 Corinthians that Paul has a very specific meaning in mind. Paul is clear on what it means to "proclaim the gospel as free of charge." To be commissioned to give his life for the cause meant he was called to be a truth-teller. The truth which he was compelled to teach is epitomized, for example, in Romans 8.

Recently I was interviewed for a newspaper article on my two-hundredth book, *Sex in the Bible*. At the end of the interview the journalist asked me what I wanted my legacy to be. Before I realized what I was saying I blurted out, "I am a truth-teller." That really does say it for me. For Paul to tell the truth, to be commissioned to proclaim the gospel, meant to emphasize the unique and unconditional grace of God. He does this nowhere as well as in Romans 8 and in our text for today. Paul had to proclaim this truth over against the prevailing religious mood and understanding of his day: the teaching of Torah with all its laws and regulations for making oneself right with God.

There was a great risk for Paul in being a truth-teller. The prevailing notion about God in his day was that God would love you if you did the right thing. God would love you if you held your mouth right, if you stood for the right things. God would love and bless you if you obeyed the prescriptions of the Torah: the Ten Commandments and the 613 additional regulations the Pharisees had built as a hedge around the Decalogue. If you obeyed God's law you could count on God's love.

Paul understood that the epitome of the gospel as revealed in Christ was in radical contrast to that. He knew that when he stood up to proclaim the gospel it was his job to say that the Torah *tradition* was in error. It was not just inadequate—it was wrong! It was incomplete. It failed to honor its own Abrahamic traditions, as Jesus claimed. It had lost its clearheaded realization that God is a God of radical, unconditional, and universal forgiveness for every human being, in spite of human behavior or character. Our relationship with God depends exclusively upon God's covenant promise of unconditional grace for all humanity, as made clear in Genesis 12 and 17.

Our behavior in life is wholesome and authentic if it is a spontaneous response of gratitude to God for God's grace. It is not authentic if we busy ourselves with the perfectionism of adherence to the law. Godliness is constituted exclusively by faith in the radical and unconditional gift of God's grace. The point of it all is simple. Anyone who really gets this experience of God's forgiving embrace of us, despite our flawed and messy inadequate lives, will inevitably turn and say, "If God feels that way about me I want to be God's kind of person!" Godly behavior is a response of gratitude to the experience of God's amazing grace.

Great pastors and preachers in the Christian tradition have always felt called and commissioned as truth-tellers. Many have had the courage to follow through and actually tell the truth as they perceived it, no matter which way it cut. Henry Ward Beecher always kept himself aware of a little sign he found when walking into a pulpit early in his preaching career. The custodian had glued the note to the inside of the pulpit. It read, "We would see Jesus!" That is a quote from the Bible story in which the Greeks came to see Jesus in Capernaum. "We would see Jesus!" Beecher, a noted preacher, said that struck him with the urgency and the weightiness of what he was up to in the pulpit. That always kept before his mind the importance of his commission as a proclaimer of the gospel, a truth-teller.

I think, though, that Richard Baxter was closer to the truth at the end of his life of ministry when he said that every time he entered the pulpit he felt that he was to preach as never sure to preach again; as a dying man to dying men! I have never entered the pulpit for the 60 years of my ministry without that sentence ringing in my mind. "Preach as never sure to preach again, as a dying man to dying men." What do dying men say? They tell

As a Dying Man

the truth! Have you not noticed the reports in the media about how some criminal in his dying moments just could not wait to bare his soul and spill all his secret knowledge about some awful crime? Sometimes it is a truth made up for heroic effect, such as the fellow who said he knew where Jimmy Hoffa was buried on the farm in Waterford, Michigan. For criminals it is usually a truth about reality long hidden and long lied about.

Dying men want to tell the truth while the light lasts. Good men want to tell the truth that saves, heals, and sets things right, while they have a chance. Good preachers and pastors, under the urgency of the commission of the gospel, want to tell the truth of God with a sense of, "Woe is me if I tell not the truth!" That urgency is appropriate to the weightiness of the gospel message that we have.

Now the church is not always ready to hear the truth. I am a truth-teller. That means I have to tell the truth, as I understand it, no matter which way it cuts. Sometimes that is comforting and comfortable; sometimes it is exasperating to parishioners. My job is to comfort the afflicted and afflict the comfortable. I am commissioned to be a truth-teller. *Woe is me if I am not a truth-teller!* The truth is God's good news of unconditional grace. Now that seems simple enough. It proves, nonetheless, to be fairly complicated.

All of us would like to endorse that simple sign Beecher saw in his pulpit, "We would see Jesus." However, there is a complexity about that. Jesus is not here. Jesus is gone. We have Jesus' story, but not Jesus. It is important that we have his story and it is important that we keep telling his story, because that story certainly conveys the essence of what Jesus was up to. It affirms what God is up to. But let us remember that the age of Jesus, in God's grand historical drama, was from 5 BCE to Pentecost. For all these centuries, we have longed so much to keep him alive in the church that we have made an idolatry of his story. His memory has too often been turned into a kind of magical mantra through which it is difficult to actually see God.

The average Christian today cannot get past the conceptual framework of that story in order to see God, the God of creation, providence, and grace. We are so easily preoccupied today, for example, with a very superficial notion of Jesus. That is the notion that Jesus is our redeemer by being a grand example for human emulation. People wear bracelets saying, "What would Jesus do?" Well, in this complicated day and age he probably would not have the slightest idea what to do, in many cases. Jesus himself said there were a lot of things he just did not know about. Only God knew those things. He worked with what was before him in his environment. That is what it meant for him to be incarnated as a human being. That is to say, Jesus was a man of the first century CE in whom God was epitomized and present to human history in that age. The age of Jesus ended at Pentecost.

The age of God as The Divine Spirit began at Pentecost and until now we live in the age of the Spirit in the church and in the world. We have been so preoccupied with a kind of idolatrous notion of Jesus' story that we have forgotten what Jesus said in his farewell address to the disciples. In John 14 he said, "I am going away. You cannot come. I will prepare mansions in heaven for you. In the meantime I will not leave you orphaned. God in the mode of the Divine Spirit will infuse your spirits. The Divine Spirit will testify about me and will lead you into all the truth."

Paul says that the presence of God in the church is the presence of the *Spirit* of Christ. This is not the age of God as present in Jesus. This is the age of God in the world as The Divine Spirit. The church has largely ignored the spirit for seventeen centuries. Occasional attempts were made to understand and recover a sense of the presence of the spirit. John Owen wrote a massive tome on the Holy Spirit in the days of the Puritans. It has been virtually ignored in favor of preoccupation with our story, creeds, theology, and propositions about Jesus. Karl Barth, the greatest Reformed Theologian of the twentieth century wrote one volume on the Holy Spirit, in his massive *Church Dogmatics*. Theologians read his volumes on Christology and ignore his work on the Holy Spirit.

Frankly, the church has always been afraid of dealing with the Divine Spirit—afraid of the theology of the Spirit, afraid of the Holy Spirit. We have been afraid of trying to figure out how to be open to the Spirit. The church has always been unsure as to how to handle the experience of the Spirit. What if the Holy Spirit blew through this church like a flame of fire and a mighty wind, as at Pentecost? How would we deal with that? What would it look like? What should we expect from it? Would any of us be ready to receive that? At the very least it would be remarkably unfamiliar to us all, would it not?

Do we have any kind of framework within which to understand that God would be acting in a mighty way with us in our day? We would quickly rush back to the Bible and read passages in the gospel, trying to bring that dramatic experience of the spirit back into line with our propositions about Jesus. Propositions about Jesus are important. The story of the gospels is peerless. We need to discern how to be open to the presence and operation of the Divine Spirit as the present day presence and action of God in the church and the world.

There was an important moment in early church history involving the eminent theologian, Tertullian. He was a lawyer from North Africa. He was the leading thinker in the church in the late second and early third century. He carefully worked out the precise technical language of the belief statements of the church. With consummate accuracy he nailed down the propositions of Christian belief. In the first four centuries the church experienced a great variety of expressions of Christian faith. Many denominations developed. Each was trying to manifest, in one way or another, the meaning of the essential Christian faith and the presence of God in the church. This produced a great variety of liturgies, life styles, belief statements, and modes of being Christian.

The bishops became fearful that the dynamics of people following the Divine Spirit would destabilize the church. So they imposed a regulation. They said that the great variety of denominations and expressions of the Spirit needed to cease. Unity and uniformity needed to be created. They decreed that the only authentic form of Christian teaching, life style, and interpretation of scripture was that prescribed and taught by the bishops. Tertullian said that they had just then organized the Holy Spirit right out of the church. So he left orthodox Christianity and joined the Montanists, spiritually a rather wild assembly, but one which emphasized being open to the presence and manifestations of God as Spirit. They were declared heretical but Tertullian liked the fact that they championed the individual experience of God's Spirit present to and apprehended by our spirits.

We have tended to intellectualize and codify the story of Jesus in the creeds, in our theological formulations, and in faith propositions for the last seventeen centuries. That codification can be useful. We would not want to discard it, but it has quenched the Spirit. We have done that because we feel much more comfortable when we have everything under control. When we intellectualize our faith and formulate it in rational propositions we feel like we have more stability. The church has always been afraid of things getting un-controlled. The uncontrollability of God as The Divine Spirit has kept the church closed to the unpredictable movements of that Spirit. Because we have defended ourselves against the presence of the Spirit, we do not experience it. Because we do not allow ourselves to experience it, we stay perpetually unsure of how to recognize the presence of the Spirit. Thus we do not know what to do with the Divine Spirit if we sense its presence in our spirits.

What do you think I should do if one of you stood up during the worship service and said to me, "I think the Holy Spirit is speaking to me and I perceive that God's Spirit is saying such and such to me"? As your pastor, what should I do? Well, I tend to take those things with cautious seriousness. I actually believe in that stuff and I would likely tell you so. What the church has done for the last seventeen centuries is to say in effect, "That cannot be right because it does not fit our creeds and book of order." But what if the Holy Spirit should be saying something new, interesting, exciting, or dynamic, to one of us present here as God's people?

The church is perpetually afraid of that idea because the Spirit cannot be canned in our theological formulations. Jesus said it plainly and without apology. He said you must be born of the Spirit. However, "the Spirit blows where it wishes. You hear the sound of it. You can see the effects of it. But you have no clue as to where it came from or where it is going" (John 3:8). Jesus and Paul both regularly enjoined us to live by the Spirit. That means they both felt that the Christian life is an intensely existential way of living. You cannot preset the leading of the Spirit. You simply have to live every day with the exciting intrigue of watching how the Spirit will show up around the next corner. If you have the eyes to see and ears to hear, the Spirit always does show up.

Now that is an exciting way to live. Why would the church be afraid of living by the Spirit? The Bible enjoins us, in both the Old and New Testaments, to such a way of life. Life in the spirit is very unpredictable. Moreover, since we as the Christian community have not cultivated the experience of living by the Divine Spirit, and are instead constrained by our doctrinal prescriptions, we have no base line for understanding when and how the Spirit is present to us.

So if you stand up in our worship to say that you have a word from the Divine Spirit, I want to hear it. However, it will make the congregation very uncomfortable. We are not used to having a word from the Divine Spirit. Of course, if you come into my counseling office and say, "You know, I think the Holy Spirit is speaking to me through the radio and telling me to burn down my neighbor's house when he is at work," I will suggest that you sound psychopathological. If you should say something else that fits squarely within the rubrics of the standard diagnostic criteria for psychosis, I will tell you that it is a mental health problem and not the Divine Spirit.

However, it is easy to tell the difference. If your message is constructively life-changing it is of the Spirit. If it is destructive it is definitely not of the Spirit. However, the point I wish to make is plain. We have the standards well worked out for abnormal behavior of specifically pathological types, and we can distinguish that very well from personal sensations of the healthy leading of God.

I said that the church has been anxiety-laden about working with these careful distinctions and, therefore, has been afraid to be open to personal experiences of Spirit-led conviction or discernment. We need to affirm the intimations of the Divine Spirit to the individual Christian and to the Christian community in its communal discernment. C. S. Lewis thought that our hesitancy in this was a serious problem for the believing community. He said we should all cultivate an openness to the *inklings* of the Spirit. I like that phrase, the *inklings* of the Spirit.

If you have been around the church for a while, a believer reading the Bible for years, there comes a point at which you have surprising spiritual discernments. These are the testimonies to your heart of the leadings and insights of God as Spirit. Most of the time you will sense how those insights line up with what you have always known and believed. Occasionally you will have the experience of an insight that can only be called a new and true illumination of God as Spirit. It affords you a brand new way of looking at things, even at the faith you have always held.

It is important to be open to the way of the Spirit with you, me, and each other. We must learn to trust the inklings of the Spirit in the church and in ourselves. We know that God is present to us in creation. We know that God is present to us in Jesus and his story. We must learn to see how God is present to us in our age, which is the age of God as Spirit. "I will not leave you orphaned," said he, "I will send to you the Holy Spirit of God. The Spirit shall lead you into all the truth" (John 14:15–16).

Jesus was not afraid to trust the rest of history to the Divine Spirit. Why should we be? If we are truth-tellers, if we are *to be* truth-tellers and hearers of the truth, we must be open to trust our own experience as a manifestation of God. We have been seasoned in the faith for a long time. We should be able to trust our own spiritual experience as the testimony of the Spirit in us. We should be glad to receive the intimations of the Spirit personally, as manifestations of the presence to us of God as Spirit. Whenever we sense such intimations we must say, "It is of the spirit." Christians are often afraid to be evangelistic. We think we must make an arduous project of it.

Actually, if we let the Spirit lead it becomes a very natural thing. Someone meets you in the grocery store and tells you a story of some meaningful thing that has happened to her. All you need to say is, "I think that is of the Spirit!" I often find myself saying to believers and non-believers, "That sounds providential to me. I believe in that stuff. I think it is of the Spirit." The response is often thoughtful and reflective.

All we need to do is to keep on saying, "I think that is of the Spirit," every chance we get. Let us keep saying that until it becomes the refrain of our lives. Say it everywhere, wherever it seems appropriate. Say it to all of your constructive experiences. "I think it is of the Spirit." If it is not, the Spirit will eventually let you know with a newer insight. We are invited to be open to that sense of interaction with God's presence constantly. It does not just happen when you read the Bible or worship in church. Let us be perpetually open to the Spirit.

The great nineteenth-century German theologian, Friedrich Schleiermacher, thought there were two aspects to discerning how the Spirit of God manifests itself to us. First, personal perceptions, inklings, intimations, and notions happen to us that testify to the grace of God actually happening in noticeable ways in our lives. You have felt such moments becoming a reality for you. Secondly, Schleiermacher thought that the Divine Spirit was manifested in those feelings we have that link us into a cherishing and charitable community of faith.

If the Divine Spirit is the soul of the church and the church is the body of the Divine Spirit it is certainly appropriate to think that we experience the spirit in those feelings that unite us in a cherishing community of faith and love. These two notions of Schleiermacher also dominate Paul's entire epistle of I Corinthians. Throughout the epistle, Paul equates the gospel of Christ with the experience of the Spirit. The entire epistle is not about Jesus. It is about Jesus' story as it is conveyed to us by the testimony of the Divine Spirit in the church.

As the presence of the Divine Spirit becomes more and more a part of your personal self-consciousness, try to be open to experiencing increasingly what it means to be the body of the Divine Spirit incarnated in you for the world. We can profit greatly from talking about the power and presence of the Spirit in the church. That is important because the church is the instrument of the Spirit. The church is the body of the spirit and the Spirit is the soul of the body, which is the community of faith. Every church is a church of the Divine Spirit. Let us open ourselves to the full scope of what that means. When we see the evidence of the presence of God as Spirit let us say to each other, "I think it is of the Spirit!" Let us make that our constant refrain! If we have the eyes to see and the ears to hear God will be present to us as the Spirit in a palpably powerful way. Pentecost is still alive in the twenty-first century, as you must know, trying to create in us a culture of the spirit!

Amen. So let it Be!

SERMON EIGHT

By the Skin of Our Teeth
—Romans 12:2, 12:21

> Be not conformed to this world but be transformed by the renewing of your minds so that you may be able to demonstrate or prove what the perfect will of God is. Do not be overcome by evil but overcome evil with good.
>
> —ROMANS 12:2, 21

BARBARA TUCHMAN WAS A fine American historian. She wrote a book entitled, *A Distant Mirror*. In that book she compared the fourteenth century with the twentieth century and said that it was remarkable how similar the key aspects of the two centuries really were. The fourteenth century was devastated by the plague and wars in Europe and resulted in a major loss of European population. As a result there was a great deal of chaos and the worst tragedy of it was a large number of orphaned children. The church and the heads of government of northern Europe forcefully stepped into the middle of that chaos, to reestablish European family and social structures.

A family structure was imposed by the authorities. It is the kind we still have today: ceremonies for marriage, both civil and ecclesiastical licenses for marriage, and very significant legal consequences in state and church government for any failures to maintain responsible social behaviors. It was an attempt to reestablish social order in the face of all of the death and loss from war and plague that had disrupted the society. The authorities imposed this social structure to give a place and means for caring for the people who were disestablished and disassociated by the chaos of the time.

Tuchman pointed out that one of the main similarities between the twentieth century and the fourteenth century was the general disaffection from the church and its authority. This had to be re-imposed by legal authority in order to maintain the social order. Tuchman's main point was that in a time of unbelievable social chaos, what saved civilization in the fourteenth century were the actions taken by the institutional church. This was not the first time that had happened. At the fall of the Roman Empire in the fifth century, it was the church as an organization and institution that maintained some semblance of order in the society while the barbarian hordes were overrunning the Empire. Ultimately it was the church that converted the Germanic hordes, incorporating them into a civilized and ordered Christianized society.

Again, in the ninth century after Christ, it was the monks of Ireland who sent missionaries from their monastic enclaves into the chaotic world of continental Europe. Those monastic missionaries reestablished Christianity there and saved Western civilization. Read Thomas Cahill's delightful book, *How the Irish Saved Civilization*. Lord Kenneth Clark, in *Civilisation*, said that "the Irish monks saved western civilization by the skin of its teeth."

It is surprising, therefore, that in the last half of the twentieth and the early years of the twenty-first century, one of the characteristics of the twentieth century that is like the fourteenth century is the general disaffection from the institutional church. Tuchman considers this a sizeable issue.

Whenever I go to the grocery store, drug store, or gas station, or wherever I encounter people socially, I usually find occasion to say something about the Christian faith. People ask me what I do. When I tell them, a conversation begins. I have been impressed for the last 30 years by the fact that almost always people respond, "Well I don't have much interest in organized religion." My response always is "Well I cannot imagine why you would prefer disorganized religion." After a while they realize that they do not mean what they say. They do not mean that they are against organized religion. They are against the institution of the church. They may be for spirituality. They may be for biblical story. They may want to preserve values that come from their heritage, but they are disaffected from the institution of the church. They want some kind of free form of spirituality that does not impose much upon them in terms of specific responsibilities or doctrinal perspective.

Now it is true, of course, that there are problems as well as virtues associated with the church as an institution throughout history. That is true of all institutions of religion. One of the great difficulties for the human race is the fact that children in each new generation have to start over morally, spiritually, and educationally, where their parents started twenty to forty years before them. Children cannot stand upon the shoulders of their parents or the previous generation on any of those things that really count. When it comes to making better cars and refrigerators we can stand upon the shoulders of the previous generation, but in terms of things spiritual, moral, and intellectual we all have to start the odyssey again at the beginning. That is a very inefficient business but it is also a wonderful business because it has everything in the world to do with the fact that human life is about freedom and growth.

However, the net result of that fact is that parents can learn everything in the world about the value of the institutions of society, and children in their adolescent enthusiasm for individuating from parents can easily try to burn all that down or feel disaffected from their parents' values. Institutionalized religion throughout history has been guilty of terrible mistakes and atrocities as well as great good and high achievements. In any case, out of that whole mix one thing has to be said constantly, namely, that in the Western World at least civilization was repeatedly saved specifically by the fact that the church was an institution. If it had not been for the institutional structure of the church, the memory and the heritage of the Christian faith and of civilizing values would not have been remembered and would not have been carried forward. Despite that, of course, there is a great world of truth in the fact that the church has made terrible errors.

Another book by Barbara Tuchman, one of my favorite authors, is *The March of Folly*. In it she claims justifiably that the church as an institution, like political organizations and societies as institutions, tends to pursue policies that initially seem to be good for it, but then continues to pursue those policies long after they become unfruitful, even counterproductive. They drive them into the ground until they become remarkably self-defeating. Tuchman claims that the Vietnam War was such a thing. So was the policy of George III that produced the Revolutionary War and American Independence. Vietnam was a good cause in the right place at the right time, but the war was won in 1968 and should have been concluded immediately in Paris at the Peace Talks, desperately sought by the North Vietnamese. However, war was continued until the policy became self-defeating for the United States and for everybody else involved. It finally ended in shame and defeat. Probably Barbara Tuchman is right about the life- cycle of institutions.

Most of you are too young to remember the Presbyterian Church undertaking in the 1960s and 70s the perfectly legitimate and necessary enterprise of intervening aggressively for social welfare and justice in our society. However, it then pushed that thing until we dumped tens of thousands of dollars into the support of Angela Davis, the leader of a communist enterprise in the USA. The abortive policy proved to be both embarrassing and wasteful for our church.

Erik Erikson wrote a book, *Young Man Luther*. In it he said that Martin Luther had the right idea but because of his bucolic and constipated personality, his aggressive motivation, and explosive style he precipitated a rift in the church that in the end was more destructive than constructive. If we had just followed Erasmus instead, the church would have been both healthier and renewed at the same time.

In any case, I want to highlight the fact that over the long wash of the ages it has consistently been the institution of the church, in spite of all the deficits that all of us feel about it, that has sustained and carried the memory of Christian civilized values. In spite of the fact that we would rather talk about the church in terms of the community of faith or the organism of believers in communion than in terms of the church as institution, for twenty centuries it has been the institutional church that has preserved the values and the civilized nature of the humane society that we all prize. I am still for the church because it is the only institution that still intends, at least, to hold out for truth and righteousness in our ethically chaotic world.

There is an interesting quote in a book recently published by a friend of mine, in which he cites a prayer that was found in the concentration camp at Ravensbruck after the defeat of the Nazis. The concentration camp was the site of an estimated ninety-two thousand men, women, and children exterminated by the Nazis. On a piece of wrapping paper found on a dead child after the camp was liberated, was this prayer:

> Oh Lord, remember not only the men and women of good will, but also those of ill will. But, do not only remember the ill will that they inflicted upon us; remember the fruits we bore, thanks

> to the suffering; the growth we got from our pain. Remember our comradeship which grew from it, our loyalty, our humility, the courage, the generosity, the greatness of heart which has grown out of all this suffering. And, when they come to judgment, those who are of ill will, let all the fruits which we have born be their forgiveness.

(Pastor Julia, "Ravensbruck Prayer," *RevGalBlogPals* (blog), May 6, 2013, http://revgalblogpals.blogspot.com/2013/05/monday-prayer-ravensbruck-prayer.html)

Think of how, in the face of the hellishness of this world, this prayer salvages the values that come only from the spirituality of the believing community. It was that redeeming spirit, constantly kept alive by the values championed in the institutional church and synagogue that has preserved authentic spirituality and genuine civilization through all the chaos and experimentation of the ages. That redeeming spirit saved us through all the evil that afflicted humanity throughout the last twenty centuries. To this spirit Paul speaks in our text. "Be not conformed to this world, but be transformed by the renewing of your minds, that you may discern and demonstrate what is the good and acceptable and perfect will of God. Be not overcome by evil, but overcome evil with good" (Romans 12:2, 12:21).

There are many things about the Christian church over time, and in our present moment, that I could lecture endlessly about while emphasizing the destructive side of church history. Nonetheless, I am for the church. I am for the church in spite of itself. I am for the church because the church is the one institution that holds out, in spite of everything, for truth, righteousness, justice, love, and beauty, in the face of a very difficult flow of human history. The believing community is the only healthy tissue in the sick body of humanity and without it we could not continue.

In Ann Weems's, *Family Faith Stories* she says,

> I've never understood those who say that they don't need the church. Mine is a profound need to worship and to live in solidarity with the community of the faithful. Of course I can pray by myself, but it has to be in the context of the covenant that you and I have with God; to love mercy in the midst of the unmerciful, to do justice in the jaws of injustice, to be humbly aware of God's grace takes constant communion with God and the community. To be faithful assumes life in this community which Christ called his church. To me the church is home.
>
> (Louisville: Westminster John Knox, 1985)

Faith and the institutional presence in the witness and structure of the church is the only long term stabilizer for a decent world. Are we at the place in the twenty first century at which it is once again "by the skin of our teeth" that we shall get through? I've often thought of what it means that in the eleventh through the fourteenth centuries, when the world was enduring degrading chaos, the north Europeans were building the great cathedrals. What does that mean? Where was that power and energy coming from? The world was losing its grip and the church was building those incredible symbols of faith, beauty, and transcendence; permanent professions of faith wrought in stone in the midst of a very bad time. Only the inspiration of the church empowered simple human hearts that cared more for the world, for the spirit, and for beauty than for themselves. They expressed that care by caring for the church that cared for the world.

These grand testimonies to the towering power of the church inspired faith and hope. Those suffering people must have felt that it was worth the trouble. What a sense of hope! The believing community transcends the common wash, ferment, chaos and cultural demeaning that is always lurking around the edges of human life and society. The believing community and its institutions are the healthy tissue in the sick body of humanity. "Be not conformed to this world, but be transformed by the renewing of your minds that you may discern and do what is the good and perfect will of God. Be not overcome by the evil that always lurks around the corner and tries to permeate our value systems and our lives. Overcome evil with good."

As I have said, I believe in the church. I believe in the church despite its humanness. I believe in the church as the community, organism, and institution. It is the institution that holds in place the polar star for the world's spiritual compass. Nothing else possesses that magnetic power of the Divine Spirit. I believe in the Holy Spirit: the holy catholic or universal church, the communion of saints . . .

Amen. So let it Be!

SERMON NINE

A Weeping God!
—John 11:35

> Jesus wept.
>
> — JOHN 11:35

JESUS WEPT! DOES GOD weep? Every year in September we are all aware of the anniversary date of the American tragedy of September 11, 2001 Like the slogan, "Remember Pearl Harbor" and before it, "Remember the Lusitania" or, "Remember the Maine," 9/11 will be forever imprinted on the minds of Americans and probably of the world.

When I think of that moment that leaves us sad and bewildered it reminds me of a wise word from John F. Kennedy. He said, "Life is a tragic adventure" and in the end he lived out that aphorism. I frequently find the occasion to use his words in pastoral counseling or clinical therapy. None of us gets clean away from the fact that all of life and every life is a tragic adventure and, therefore, it is all the more interesting that the gospel should have bothered to record a story in which the most gripping words are those two: "Jesus wept."

A Weeping God!

Of course the whole Bible is full of that tragic underside of life's story. Job certainly thought that life was a tragic adventure and he spent thirty-six chapters in his book wrestling with the fact that he could make no sense of it. His four friends spent the same amount of time trying to hold on to their denial of the fact. They were quite certain that life is a tragic adventure only for the wicked but they were, of course, badly wrong. It is true for everyone and no one escapes.

I have prayed daily for many years that God would deliver me, my parishioners, my patients, and my family from the painful ordeal of living life's suffering. God has not done so. God has done something about it but God has not delivered us from it. It is a rare circumstance in which we can remember an occasion when suffering or tragedy struck and God delivered us from it. In my life prayer has never produced deliverance from life's ordeal of suffering. My experience has always been that instead God has interpreted it to me. God has often given me spiritual and emotional growth through my suffering. Even so, that has always proved to be painful and arduous.

As a result I resent the fact that we have to work so hard to keep life in reasonable order and acceptable safety. I resent that we have to work so hard to get constructive and tangible growth out of our pain. That is, I chafe under the reality that one has to be so excruciatingly thoughtful, careful, and responsible just to perceive meaning in the process of life's unfolding and to take the kind of risks that are necessary in order to go on courageously in the face of the tragic nature of life. As a result, there are a lot of people who really see life as though "the glass is half empty." We deal with people like that all the time. They are *only able to see* that life is a tragic adventure. That is not surprising. Some even seem to settle for getting a certain kind of gratification out of being preoccupied with the negative and with their suffering. They give the impression that it makes quite a heroic story for them.

Jesus wept, but he saw a lot of constructive excitement about life, nonetheless. The tradition of Jesus' community of faith, the ancient Israelites, was a long tradition of tragic adventure. Nonetheless, when we read Psalms we notice that at least half of them celebrate life. They recall how God visited and delivered the Psalmist's ancestors. Indeed, sometimes when trying to hang on to a constructive perspective, the Psalmist exaggerates divine deliverance. Read Psalm 136 for example. It is a long litany of deliverances of Israel. However, if you read the actual record from Exodus and Deuteronomy to 2 Chronicles, things were not quite that rosy while they were actually experiencing their ordeal. There was something about that Israelite tradition that rejected the conclusion that life is ultimately and only tragic. Those folks worked hard for the persistence of hope.

Moreover, Job had a difficult struggle with the meaning of the relationship between suffering and God's providence in our lives. Nonetheless, he continued to say that if he could only talk to God about his suffering, he was certain that God would have a sensible way to account for it. In the end, however, Job concluded that though he searched in every way, he could not find God in his pain. God was silent until the very end of the story.

The Epistle to the Hebrews enjoins us in chapters 11 and 12 that we should pray confidently. The writer casts that notion in the context of the gospel story. That gospel story is mainly the narrative about the wonderful way in which Jesus handled people. The intent of the gospel is to get across to us that God handles people as Jesus did. Of course, the gospel writers were conscious that this was important. People need to hear that kind of story about God, because it is not always readily apparent in everyday experience. The story in the gospels and the message of Hebrews tries to inform us that at the very least the glass of life is half full, not half empty. That is, in the face of the tragic adventure of life there is reason for a certain, steady, and sturdy optimism about things. To put it differently, Hebrews is all about hope.

Now most of us understand what faith means. We know that faith means to trust God for God's goodness, grace, and providence in our lives even when things do not necessarily look so good and gracious and provident. That is, faith is a way of taking the long view in terms of the palpable evidence we do have of the good providence and healing grace of God. That is what Hebrews enjoins us to do and it speaks in terms of Christian hope.

Now hope, according to John Calvin, is faith projected into the unknown of the future, the infinite unknown from here to eternity. That is, hope is not, "I hope that will happen." That is a kind of a tentative childish desire that our wishes will be fulfilled. That is not what we mean by Christian hope. Christian hope is a certain and sturdy confidence, according to Calvin, that what we hold in faith can be held throughout all the unknown of life's future. Whether things look like the glass is half full or half empty in and of themselves, in any given moment in life, we can confidently go forward into the unknown certain that God will always be for us in our hope, what God has always been for us in our faith.

Hebrews and the gospels enjoin us to cast our life's adventure in terms of that sense of trust in God that makes our assurance of the future secure

A Weeping God!

in spite of whatever may come. My experience has been that God does not deliver us from suffering. I no longer expect that God will deliver me from suffering. I expect, for example, that there is a good chance that if I live long enough I will need to have another heart surgery. I just happen to have the kind of constitution that about every 18 years things plug up no matter what I do. I do not think God is going to deliver me *from* that, but my experience has been that God delivers me *through* life's suffering. God delivers me *to something* not *from something*. In all my personal suffering God has delivered me to growth and to seasoning. God has given me a great sense of gratitude and the peace that comes from that experience.

That sense of things is on a much higher order than we would ever have if God simply eliminated suffering from us. We grow and are seasoned through our suffering. It drives us into the deep resources of spiritual strength inside ourselves where God's spirit is lively. God does not cause our pain but God enters into it to make of our wreckage the fertilizer that causes flowers to grow in our lives.

It is interesting that the text, "Jesus wept," is in the middle of the story of Lazarus's death. That is a peculiar story. Peculiar in terms of what it says about Jesus. Jesus was in Galilee and Lazarus was in Bethany near Jerusalem. Jesus got the word that Lazarus was sick. Jesus hung around in Galilee for a number of days. He did not rush off to Bethany until the message came that Lazarus had died. Then he went slowly to Bethany and he got there a week or so after Lazarus was buried. When he talked to Mary and Martha, Mary said, "Lord if you had just come on time he wouldn't have died"(John 11:35). Jesus did not respond to that except that Jesus wept.

What was he weeping about and why did he not get there on time and save Lazarus? What is the enigma in that story that we are supposed to see? Was it that he could not prevent Lazarus' death? Well maybe. Maybe he could not deliver Lazarus from the tragedy. However, the story says he raised him from the dead. That's a pretty good trick. You would think that you would want to take preventive steps which might be a lot easier, but he did not. Mary was asserting that an ounce of prevention would have been better than a pound of cure. Instead he stood there and wept.

He apparently had the power to prevent the tragedy. He could have delivered his loved ones from that suffering. Instead he is anguished about the death. What does that mean? What does that say to us about God? What are we to make of that? Did Mary and Martha need the tragedy? Did Lazarus need it? Was it an advantage for Lazarus to come back from the dead and have to do it all over again 10 years later? That does not sound like a good idea. It is a strange and interesting story, is it not? What are we to make of God's healing style in this strange narrative?

I do not think that the writer intends by his story to raise those kinds of questions. I think what he intends to say is, "Jesus wept." That is, whatever God could do, might do, or wished to do about our tragedy, God, actually works with us in such a way that God enters into our suffering with us. The process of the human condition, which for us sometimes becomes a great anguish, is for God an equal source of anguish. God weeps with us. Our life is a tragic adventure for God, too. That is why the scripture enjoins us to weep with those who weep and rejoice with those who rejoice.

The message of the gospel in this passage is designed to say that God is our co-pilgrim in the pilgrimage of life. That is a whole lot more consolation and a much greater source of strength and meaning than if we had some sort of magical God whose business was to prevent tragedy from happening. A magical God would not be very personal. A God of pathos, a God who can weep, a God who enters as a fellow pilgrim into our journey, is a personal God. With such a God we can endure and savor the flavor of life's experiences and get the growth and meaning that comes only that way–from pain.

I think that we grow only from our pain. Pleasure is delightful, but it focuses us outside of ourselves to things and experiences *out there*. It draws us out into entertainments and distractions. Suffering drives us into the center of ourselves where we discover the resources we have in our core personalities. Suffering opens to us our own real selves and gives us an opportunity to see our inner spirituality and the strengths and the power of God's Spirit there within us. We cannot see these insights in the distractions of our entertainments and our pleasures. God enters into both pain and pleasure with us, of course, but I think that God knows that if God were to constantly manipulate the human process to straighten things out for us and protect us from reality, the integrity of our own human nature would be violated. Moreover, we could not get the experience of growing up spiritually with God. It is the destiny and role of the human pilgrimage to produce growth in us.

Jesus did not rush there and prevent Lazarus's death. He went there and wept with those who were experiencing the profound loss. He experienced the loss as his loss and then in the end, he helped them through it. One does not want to make much of that resurrection of Lazarus because it is a very ambiguous story. I think if Jesus had asked Lazarus if he had wanted to go through that again, Lazarus would have turned him down. So the story is not about raising Lazarus from the dead. The resurrection of Lazarus, whether it was symbolic or literal, is about the fact that God delivers us *through* the travail of human suffering. God is a pilgrim with us in our pilgrimage. God weeps with those who weep and rejoices with those who rejoice. Jesus wept about the kind of travail human life always is. Jesus wept about us, with us, and for us

The event of September 11 2001 was real evil. As in the case of all evil it was the evil of humans against humans. The issue is not whether God was behind it or God could have prevented it. The issue is, how does God enter into something like that, and how can we see God coming in it? That's the issue! Jesus did not prevent Lazarus's death, but he did deliver his loved ones from their grief through the process of that suffering and the growth they derived from it.

Where is God in all of that? Well, it depends on what kind of God you are looking for. If we are looking for a God of magic deliverance, no such God exists. If we are looking for a God who is an insurance policy against suffering, that God does not exist. If we are looking for a providential escape hatch from the normal adventure of life, however beautiful or tragic, there is no God to fit that requirement. Those gods of the past are dead.

Some people feel that God is nowhere around. I suppose that those who were on the top floor of the World Trade Center in that conflagration of September 11 may very well have felt that. As Jesus did on the cross when he cried out, "My God, my God, why have your forsaken me?" (Mark 15:34) If we are looking for the God of consolation who assists us in rebuilding or recovering through the seasoning of growth from our tragedy, then we have the God who, like Jesus' way of handling people, is a God of mercy and of grace—who weeps with those who are weeping.

Evil is human, not cosmic. Grace is divine and world-embracing. When we read that Jesus wept, we know that God weeps with us and for us. A few days before his death Jesus was weeping again. We can hear him sighing deeply, "Oh Jerusalem, Jerusalem, how often I would have gathered your children under my wings as a hen gathers her chickens, and you would not" (Matt 23:37, Luke 13:34). There Jesus stood on the Mount of Olives with his impending death before him, weeping with us and for us. *Right in the middle of those divine tears is the meaning of everything in life.* Jesus wept.

Amen. So let it Be!

SERMON TEN

The Cross as Christian Symbol
—Matthew 4:1–2, 4:8–9, 16:24–26;
1 Corinthians 1:17–18, 1:21–25

THE WORD OF THE cross is the power of God

Perhaps you have had the dubious opportunity to see the Jewish and Christian catacombs in Rome. They are underground caves, in which the ancient Jews and Christians met for worship, buried their dead, and hid from Roman persecution.

There are many things to see in the catacombs that help us understand the early development of our Christian faith. One of the surprising things is the absence of the symbol of the cross during the first three centuries of Christian history. The cross did not become a Christian symbol until around the time of Constantine at the beginning of the fourth century. Constantine is reported to have seen a vision in the sky just before the fateful battle at the Milvian Bridge. In that vision a cross appeared with an inscription in Latin reading, *In hoc signo vinces! (In this sign conquer)!* Constantine then had a cross painted upon all the shields of his soldiers and proceeded to give battle to the forces of the Western Roman Empire. He defeated them roundly and set in motion the unification of the Roman Empire, governed from Constantinople (modern Istanbul).

The Cross as Christian Symbol

That is one of the earliest recorded instances of the use of the cross as a Christian symbol. When preparing to preach on this theme, I thought immediately of the catacombs and Constantine.

We all sing with great emotion the hymn:

In the cross of Christ I glory,
Towering o'er the wrecks of time.
All the light of sacred story,
Gathers round its head, sublime.

(John Bowring, "In the Cross of Christ I Glory, 1825)

That surely seems to epitomize appropriate Christian devotion and piety. The difficulty is that the early Christians and Jesus himself would not join us in that song. They would have no idea why we create and celebrate that kind of symbolism. We wrap a great deal of theology into that hymn as its verses unfold. Its last verse, for example, says,

Bane and blessing, pain and pleasure
By the cross are sanctified.
Peace is there that knows no measure,
Joys that through all time abide.

To be celebrating so joyfully a Roman instrument of such cruelty would appall Jesus and the early Christians. Jesus hated the cross, as we know from his anguish in Gethsemane and on Golgotha. The early Christians saw it as an offense and a monstrosity. Their faith symbols were the fish, the dove, the star, the lamb, and the good shepherd. Those are the symbols that dominated the catacombs for the first three centuries. The fish derived from the Greek monogram *ICHTHUS*. That means fish. In Greek the letters were the initials of the phrase: *Iesous Christos Theou Uios Soter*: Jesus Christ, God's Son, Savior. The dove represented the Divine Spirit which Jesus had promised to send to lead the church into all the truth. The lamb and the Good Shepherd were a mixed metaphor for Jesus as the gentle rescuer who also died in his effort to save us. Jesus as the Lamb of God was celebrated as the unflinching savior whose inflexible pursuit of his ideal goals got him killed.

Most of us wear crosses as symbols of something important about us. I notice that every sort of person in our society wears a cross. Quite surprisingly, most criminals who appear on TV during newscasts are wearing crosses. Occasionally one sees a Mogen David (Star of David). When I see you wearing a cross I wonder what that means to you. What kind of statement do you mean to be making by wearing it?

For some, I sense that it is merely a piece of decorative jewelry. I think those folks are in the minority. For most I think it is intended to mean that the wearer is making some kind of religious or spiritual statement, but not necessarily Christian. When I speak with people who wear crosses, sometimes they do not know or cannot say exactly what they mean by it. However, I notice that usually people mean that they want to be publicly identified as somewhat religious. I am surprised at how often such folk do not mean by wearing it to state that they are Christians. They simply have some intention regarding God or religion.

I assume that anyone in this congregation who wears a cross does so with the specific intent of declaring thereby that he or she is a committed Christian. However, we might really think about reconsidering how good a symbol that really is for such a statement of one's faith. As I said, Jesus and the early Christians knew nothing of a cross as a Christian symbol, and they hated that symbol of Roman oppression. It came into use very late and then mainly as a way of identifying the newly Christianized empire with *The Conquering Christ*. That designation would have offended Jesus as well. He went to great pains to insist that he was the forgiving savior not the conquering Christ. Indeed, one of his three temptations in the wilderness dealt with this very option, bowing down to power and becoming the new Alexander the Great, ruler of the nations. Jesus rejected that option with vigor.

Moreover, long before Constantine, already in the first century, particularly at the first Pentecost, the early Christians associated the cross with their claim that the Jews were Christ-killers. That symbolic meaning attached itself to the cross from that first century to our own day. Pope John XXIII had to publicly and officially apologize to the entire Jewish world for the fact that Christians have denigrated, persecuted, and exterminated Jews because we accused them of *deicide*: killing God. Even if the cross has only positive meaning for us, we cannot imagine what it means to those around us who see us wearing it.

I was amazed two years ago when I was speaking to a close Jewish friend of mine about an exercise program she was seeking for her family. I urged her to go to the YMCA in Farmington. I was stunned when she said that she could not go there because they would not allow her a membership. "The YMCA is a Christian organization which represents itself that

The Cross as Christian Symbol

way to keep Jews out," she believed. Of course, that is not true, but that was her understanding, and it must be the understanding of Jews generally that we have a YMCA to keep them away from us. So they build their duplicative Jewish institutions instead. So do the Muslims, I understand.

You might feel insulted by that assumption on their part, as I did, but they have good reason to feel that way. Not only did the supposedly Christian nation of Germany go to great lengths to exterminate the Jews a half-century ago, but that has been the standard history under the symbol of the cross for seventeen hundred years. When I traveled to the Holy Land for the first time in March of 1960, I bought for my wife a lovely necklace which she still occasionally wears. It is a Crusader's Cross. Many of you have acquired the same medallion-like cross when traveling in the Near East. I did not think of the fact, at that time, that a Crusader's Cross represents a horrid tragedy perpetrated against Jews and Muslims by the Christian Crusaders of the eleventh and twelfth centuries. When preparing to march to the Holy Lands to deliver the ancient biblical sites from the "Infidel" Turks, the German Crusaders first spent an entire spring and summer ravaging all the Jewish communities in Europe. They killed as many Jews as they could catch, destroyed their habitations, and stole their money and property to finance the crusades.

Can you imagine what it means for a Jew or a Muslim to see us parading our crosses? Whether that should make a difference to us, it should make us stop and think. When I see a Jew wearing a Star of David I always assume that it means, "I am a Jew, one of those people whom you Christians have harried and hurt and hellishly abused over the centuries." I do not know if those Jewish people who wear the Mogen David have that in mind at all, but I do, and so I can imagine what a cross represents for a lot of them.

Last week I saw a film entitled, *Sister Rose's Passion*. It is about the Roman Catholic nun from a Wisconsin Dominican Order who completed her doctorate in the 1950s or 60s at St. Louis University, a Catholic institution. She was asked to do her research on a Roman Catholic Church self-study, financed by Jewish people, in which she was to find out what the Catholic Churches were teaching in their school textbooks. Her dissertation became famous for a number of reasons. The main point it revealed was the anti-Jewish teachings that dominated Catholic textbooks. She was appalled to find that all of them claimed aggressively that the Jews were despicable people who killed God and, as a result, are forced by God to wander homeless all over the face of the earth forever, and go to hell in the end. The textbooks explained that this destiny was a result of the fact that the Jews had rejected Christ as their Messiah, and so God had rejected them.

Sister Rose made it her life's work and passion to correct that. It was because of the grudging support she got from her Archbishop that she was able to file a brief to the Vatican. That became a working paper for the Second Vatican Council, in the mid-1960s. The very last action of Vatican II before it adjourned was to approve the papal decree *Nostra Aetate*. That official document forbad Catholics to say, teach, or believe that the Jews are Christ-killers or that they are cursed of God. Paul makes plain in his epistles to the Galatians, Ephesians, Colossians, and Romans that God has not and never will reject his people, the children of Abraham, Isaac, and Jacob. So we had better watch our step as well, and get in line with God! Because of the work of Sister Rose, Pope John XXIII apologized to the whole world for the whole of Christendom, for Protestants and Catholics alike. Well he should have. Sister Rose wears a composite of the cross and the Star of David, worked into one piece of jewelry.

Of course, Sister Rose had much to say, therefore, about Mel Gibson and his film, *The Passion of Christ*. She affirmed him for showing us boldly how terrible was the real suffering of Jesus Christ. She commended Mel for symbolically using his own hands in the film. His hands are on the hammer driving the nails into Jesus hands and feet. She acknowledged Mel's attempt to say symbolically, thereby, that he and you and I are responsible for killing Christ. That is, we perpetuate the kind of world in which, if you stand for what Jesus stood for, and will not back down as he would not, you will be destroyed for it. Mel was saying symbolically, "We killed Christ." We do not need to seek out the Jews for blame. Besides, the cross was not an instrument the Jews used for punishment, nor were they permitted by the Romans to crucify anyone. Only the Romans had the right and practice to crucify people.

However, Sister Rose took Mel Gibson to task for making so much of the remarks of a local mob of Jews two thousand years ago who said, "Crucify him! Crucify him! His blood be upon us and our children!" (Matt 27:25). Mel took those words, as Christians always have tended to take them and applied them to all Jews from that day to this. That motley crowd of hysteric fools two thousand years ago, who wanted Jesus done away with, did not speak for any other Jews from that time or this. Moreover, there is no certainty that the gospel report is historically accurate rather than a

The Cross as Christian Symbol

partisan report by angry and grieving followers of Jesus, trying to remember the scene fifty years later when the gospel was written. If we generalize that raucous crowd's venom and idiocy, and apply it to Jews generally, we commit a worse crime than the crucifixion of Jesus Christ.

So what about our crosses as Christian symbols? What do we mean by them? What can we mean and what should we mean? Last year we invited a Jewish scholar, Professor Ithamar Gruenwald, to our sanctuary to preach the sermon. What must it have meant to him to be delivering the word of God to us while standing beneath our towering cross? I must confess that the thought never passed through my mind until I began to write this sermon. Should we do away with the cross? Should we reinterpret it? Should we modify it somehow to change or mask its meaning?

It is interesting that at the time of the Protestant Reformation all the Reformed Churches radically modified this symbol from a crucifix to a cross. The crucifix, namely, the cross with the body of Jesus the Christ upon it, became a Christian symbol very much later than Constantine, even after the Crusades, sometime in the late Middle Ages. Martin Luther, John Calvin, and their colleagues did away with the body on the cross so that, if we were going to use a cross at all, it would be an empty cross, representing Christ resurrected. The original Reformed Churches and Presbyterian Churches forbad the use of the cross at all. Only after World War II did crosses start to become universally used in our churches as architectural, liturgical, and artistic symbols.

The issue really is, "What do we mean by the crosses we wear, or with which we are identified?" For thirty-seven years I wore a cross all the time, on my uniform as an Army Chaplain. I would be out of uniform even now if I did not wear the crosses when in uniform. In the army the cross identified me as a servant to all humankind, indeed, a person passionate about the well-being of all of God's creatures in war and peace. I stood for a saving and healing presence wherever I was. I liked that a lot! You will notice, however, that though I wear some jewelry, every piece of which has a special symbolic import in my family, you have never seen me wear a cross in civilian attire. The reason is that I am unclear what message it sends.

What message does your cross send? Does it say, "I want you all to know I am not a Jew or a Muslim?" Does it mean, "I am against Jews?" Does it mean, "I am for Christ and God's reign of *grace that works* and *love that heals*?" Do you mean to proclaim by your cross, "I am willing to give myself to the cause of Christ at some cost to myself?" Does it say what

Paul said, "I am crucified with Christ, therefore, it is no longer I who live, but Christ who lives in me?" (Gal 2:20) Does it mean, "I am prepared to put my life and wealth on the line for what Christ is for in this church and world?" Does it mean, The word of the cross is, for us who are being saved, the power of God and the wisdom of God, as in our scripture for today? (1 Cor 1:18–25)

Do you think that is the message that the Jews and Muslims in our society are getting from our symbol? How could they possibly get that message after seventeen hundred years in which the cross has been used as a sword? Obviously, we cannot just wear the cross as jewelry. Then it is an ugly monstrosity. Obviously, we cannot just wear the cross and expect others to understand what it means to us. Obviously, we cannot sing the hymn I quoted every time someone notices our crosses. The two verses I did not recite are worth noticing:

> When the woes of life o'ertake me,
> Hopes deceive, and fears annoy,
> Never shall the cross forsake me,
> Lo! It glows with peace and joy.
> When the sun of bliss is beaming
> Light and love upon my way,
> From the cross the radiance streaming
> Adds more luster to the day.

Is there any way that a Jew or Muslim could know that you attach those sentiments to your cross unless, of course, you told them at some length? But what does that hymn mean even for you and your cross?

Well, that hymn speaks of lovely nineteenth-century sentimentality; but when was the last day that the cross really meant exactly that to you? What is the chance that anyone seeing you wear it would have interpreted it that way? I am quite impatient with the abstract sentimental metaphors of a lot of our hymns. Our world today is much more literal-minded and empirically-oriented, and so is the world of those around us who see our crosses on churches or on our persons.

When Christians wear crosses with conscious intentionality, it usually means that we hold dear what Jesus Christ stood for and held dear. That seems to me to be a good and important meaning. However, I suppose the only way we can avoid unconsciously spreading a lot of poison around us with our crosses is to speak up and interpret them for exactly the constructive messages they mean to us. The cross is a very ambiguous Christian symbol at best and a horrid offense at worst, so we need to make sure that our testimony is plain, verbalized, and articulate. If you are not ready to speak up for Christ, do not wear this symbol. If you wear this symbol, keep interpreting it every chance you get. You will be surprised how that will enhance your Christian witness and create unexpected opportunities for it. Can you imagine all the wonderful conversations you will have with your Jewish and Muslim brothers and sisters, before the face of God? You might start it out by asking them what they mean by their symbols. That should break the ice. No more ice between brothers and sisters! *Never again!*

Amen. So let it Be!

SERMON ELEVEN

The Laughing Christ
—Hosea 1:1–3:1b

> God loves people. People love raisins.
>
> — Hosea 3:1b

My theme this morning is *The Laughing Christ*, and my text is Hosea 3:1b, "God loves his people, but the people prefer raisins." You remember that the most famous portrait of Jesus seen everywhere in the world where anyone pays any attention to Jesus is that wonderfully dignified but placid portrait called Warner Sallman's *Head of Christ*. We all know that picture imprinted indelibly in our minds. It has been in the minds of every generation for a couple of centuries. It is an elegant, finely crafted piece of art. Sallman's Head of Christ seems transcendent, holy, peaceful, ethereal, and godlike.

I hope you also remember that in the 1970s, an artist who was dissatisfied with the ethereal transcendence implied in Sallman's Head of Christ, painted a really hilarious portrait of Jesus laughing. His head is thrown back, his beard unkempt. He is laughing broadly—a great belly laugh. It is written all over his face, his eyes twinkling joyfully. The radical difference

The Laughing Christ

between *The Laughing Christ*, as Ellen Wallace Douglas called it, and Sallman's *Head of Christ* is the utter divinity of Sallman's Head of Christ and the utter humanness of *The Laughing Christ*. Both are true, and in the absence of either we do not have a full portrait of Jesus.

Therefore, I should like to call your attention to the fact that throughout the Bible there are attention-getting indications of the appropriateness of the portrait, *The Laughing Christ*. The Bible has a pervasive and not-so-subtle subtext portraying God as a God of great humor. Many people are offended by the suggestion that God has a sense of humor and yet unless we are willing to open ourselves to that truth we miss an entire layer of the text of the Bible. More than that we miss the essential message of the scripture regarding the radical nature of God's relationship to us and to God's world. God has a great sense of humor as well as being serious about a lot of things. Jesus' life was filled with humorous moments.

Indeed, I offer you a challenge. Whenever you are reading the story of Jesus in the gospels notice what Jesus is saying or doing in the narrative. Consider the possibility that Jesus is being humorous or teasingly ironic in what he does and says. If I drew your attention to the scripture in which he says "Suffer the little children to come unto me and forbid them not for of such is the kingdom of heaven" (Mark 10:13), neither you nor I would immediately think of that as hilarious. However, reconstruct the context for a moment. Jesus' disciples are officiously protecting him from what they consider bothersome children. They think Jesus is way too important to be mucking around with some snotty-nosed kids. They need to think that way because if he is not too important for that, then they are not nearly as important as they think they are because then they have identified themselves with a rather ordinary guy. They want to insist that he and they have divine, heavenly, transcendent business. They cannot possibly mess around with children or be distracted by them. So the disciples were busy getting them out of Jesus' hair, so to speak.

Can you imagine the crowd standing around, with the disciples in the inner circle, and noticing Jesus turning to them and saying, *What's with you guys? Who do you think I want to see, if not the children? Bring the children to me. My whole business is about children. Of such is the kingdom of heaven.* He followed that up, you remember, by setting a little child in the inner circle and saying, *If you do not take things as a little child you cannot see the kingdom breaking in around you. If you are not trusting and as simply straightforward as a child the kingdom is going to happen all around you all the time and you will not even notice it happening. The reign of God's love and grace is in the process of coming into this world. It is happening in the loving care of people all around you. You need the spirit of a child to see it. Officiousness will blind you. You will be too busy with all kinds of official stuff, academic research, or church projects, and you will not notice my real stuff happening.*

That is a hilarious story if you think about it. Jesus' entire life, I think, can be read from the perspective of an ongoing flow of humorous cracks. His life can be defined as an enterprise in puncturing people's balloons of arrogance, officiousness, and narcissism wherever he could find them. Jesus was enormously humorous and in that he was reflecting the fact that God is enormously humorous. You could read the whole Bible as God expressing his humorous take on time, history, humans, our humanness, our perplexity, our foibles, and God's ultimate solution of unconditional grace and forgiveness.

Think of the story of Hosea. I think his first three chapters are the most hilarious story in the Bible. God says to Hosea, *Go down to the red light district and get yourself a whore, and love her, care for her, marry her, and have children with her.* So Hosea does that. However, she runs away and goes back to the red light district. He goes down again at God's command and gets her back. In the process of this, which repeats itself numerous times, she gets pregnant and bears three children, none of whom are Hosea's. God gives them each a name that means that they are disowned bastards. God instructs Hosea to name them names that mean "These are not my children." God says, *This is like my relationship to Israel. This is like my relationship to my people, to all of you. I keep telling you how much I love you. I keep cherishing you. Nonetheless, you keep going down your own road with impunity.*

Nonetheless, as the drama matures and comes to the passage that is our text, what happens? God does the absolutely hilarious thing. He says, *You know what I am really going to do is this: I am going to embrace you anyway. I am going to love you anyway. You cannot possibly sin yourself out of my embrace. I am going to keep on loving you and I will declare that those children which were illegitimate children and do not belong to me are in fact mine. I do not care where they came from or how they got here, they are mine! Where it was said that you were not mine, there it shall be said, "These are Children of the Living God.*

What a hilarious turn of events. That radical event of grace in which the worst thing you could imagine, the worst story you could write, the worst behavior you could possibly carry out, cannot get you outside of God's economy of saving grace. You cannot drop yourself off the edge into the abyss of hell. You cannot find a way of escape from God's love. You cannot slip out of God's long embrace. You cannot sin yourself out of God's grace. The humor is captured in the last line of our text. "God loves his people, even though the people would rather have raisins, sweets, and candy. God loves his people but the people prefer raisins"

The story of Hosea is intended to be a radical illustration of the hilarious drama of human existence, as seen from the perspective of God. Ralph Wood wrote a book about the theology of grace in the literature of such American writers as John Updike, Peter De Vries, Flannery O'Conner and Walker Percy. He called it *The Comedy of Redemption.* You ought to read it. Hosea's story is a comedy of redemption as seen in the economy of divine grace. God is saying here, *Don't take things so seriously. Don't take yourself so seriously. Don't take your humanness too seriously. Don't take your sin too seriously. Do not take things too seriously, because no matter how serious things might be, I love you. I embrace you. I forgive you in advance. Every child, every human being who seems more like a son of Satan than like a son of God is my child. Where it was said, 'these are not my people'; there it will be said, 'Children of the Living God'*(Hos 3:1b).

Can you think of a better joke? Can you think of a more towering transcendental stroke of hilarity? Humans can perpetrate any type of unacceptable and distorted dysfunction, and the answer to it is always absolute and total forgiving grace?

One time Jesus was asked whether people should get a divorce and he gave a very simple response. He said, *It's a bad idea.* They countered, *Moses said we could get a divorce in case of adultery."* Adultery? Jesus said. *Adultery! Adultery is no harder to forgive than lust, which everyone commits all the time. Adultery is as easy to forgive as is any sin. Furthermore the only reason Moses gave you the right to get a divorce because of adultery is because you are so blockheaded that you cannot forgive like God forgives. You cannot heal like God heals.* Of course, in the end Jesus did not forbid divorce. Jesus promoted relationships that heal and grow and in which love flourishes. Nonetheless, he was intent upon puncturing a large hole in that legalistic balloon that the people standing around were trying to stuff in his face.

By Grace Alone

This is not a sermon on divorce; this is a sermon on God's humor and Jesus' hilarity. Jesus said, *God's economy is designed for forgiveness and healing. Just because you are too blockheaded to forgive does not mean that God cannot forgive and heal.* The reduction of all of that to one simple practical point comes down to this, that in God's economy we cannot beat the game and we cannot lose the game.

We cannot escape the consequences of our responsibility, but at the same time God's game is a game in which he declares us winners in spite of our irresponsibility or failures. If you drink too much for forty years, you are going to die from liver disease. All of God's forgiveness in the world is not going to prevent that. If you abuse your husband for forty years you will be a very lonely old lady. God cannot prevent that. All of God's forgiveness in the world is not going to change that. Nonetheless, you cannot lose because God will continue to embrace and bless you and say, *You know that husband-abuser in you is my forgiven child. The only thing that I can see when I look at you is that you are a saint, washed clean by my grace. You are a saint getting ready for heaven. I cannot remember that story of her beating the daylights out of her husband for forty years.*

In God's economy you cannot beat the game but you cannot lose the game either. It is a win-win game. People prefer raisins but God loves his people. The ultimate example of this in the Bible is that absolutely hilarious occasion when the priests, scribes, and Pharisees came to Jesus with all of their legalistic prescriptions. They insisted rigidly upon the laws about keeping the Sabbath and about going to the temple, the laws about making sacrifices and about giving a tithe of their income. All this was legalistic stuff they were trying to impose in order to straighten up the Israelites and bring them back to a vital life as God's people. Jesus said, *You know, this is a bad joke. Your economy is a bad joke, and God's economy is a hilarious economy, a good joke. You guys are acting like the fellow who tried to cough up a gnat and he swallowed a camel.* Can you imagine the story?

There was an Arab spice trader trekking across the dessert from Palestine to Iraq. He was leading his camel. He was all tuckered out and dried up, huffing and puffing his way through the sand. He was breathing deeply with his big mouth wide open. Suddenly a desert sand flea flew in and went straight down his dilated wind pipe. The poor guy coughed and carried on in a frenzy. He hacked and puked and could not get that sand flea out. Meanwhile, his poor camel, probably his only friend in the world, was terribly excited and concerned. So he got right up there close and looked down the Arab's big throat and saw him hacking and coughing spasmodically. The camel was trying to figure out what was the matter with his friend. Then, suddenly, with one great orgasmic gasp the Arab got the sand flea out and the camel in.

Your legalism, Jesus said, *is going to croak you. You are going to get a camel stuck in your throat, because you are preoccupied with legalistic gnats. Your method does not fit God's economy. You may remove the little flaws and failures of humankind, but you will choke on the real issues. Only grace can handle those. God's economy is a win-win game.*

People like candy instead of God. God likes people in spite of themselves. You can be a wretch, like Hosea's whore, but you cannot lose because God holds you in the hands of forgiving grace. The Jewish religious leaders did not think human dysfunction was so severe it could not be fixed with moral band-aids. Jesus thought we were all really lost from God and needed spiritual surgery—a change of heart. He knew we could only be fixed by God holding on to us in forgiveness, unconditionally, no matter what, even if we prefer the projects of this world while he deals in the eternal matters of heaven. God loves all people, even though most people prefer raisins.

Amen. So let it Be!

SERMON TWELVE

When God Moves In
—Revelations 21:1–8

> I heard a loud voice from heaven say, "Look, God lives with humans. God is making all things new!"
>
> — REVELATION 21:3, 5

THE SCRIPTURE FOR TODAY is two lines, one from the third verse and one from the fifth verse of Revelation 21. In contemporary English they read, "God's home is with humans . . . God is renovating everything."

I have a friend named Kip. He bought a used Jeep and drove it about four months, when he wrecked the front end of it. It was in the repair shop for a week. When he drove it out of the shop he was immediately hit in the rear end by another car, which did three times the damage of the original accident. Kip got out of his Jeep and walked over to the driver of the other car who was in a hysteric fit. Kip spoke to her kindly and told her that stuff happens and that he had this kind of an experience before. She was impressed by how calmly and humorously he was handling it and asked him how he could be so cool when she had just wrecked his Jeep. Kip walked over to his vehicle, reached into the front seat, picked up a copy of The

Upper Room, a Christian devotional pamphlet. He handed it to her and said "This is the only thing that works for me."

The story behind this story is that four months earlier Kip had called me in desperation. He was coming off a lost weekend of drugs and alcohol. He had hit bottom. He had lost his family, his wife, his job, and his livelihood. He was living in his car. Kip's brother and mother are devoted Christians filled with a sense of personal spirituality. They are busy church people and an incarnation of the nature of what it means to be a Christian. They had never stopped praying for Kip and loving him. Kip came in for therapy and God moved in and made everything new, renovated his inner world. That was the story that Kip was telling when he picked up *The Upper Room* saying, "This is the only thing that ever worked for me."

Some years ago, I had a reason to buy four Florida condos. The contractor had gone bankrupt and they were unfinished. I put some money into them and turned them from a disaster into extraordinarily elegant beauty and sold them at the top of the market. Renovation really can make an amazing difference. God is in the specific business of renovation. The Bible says, "God is making everything new." It worked so well on my condos that I decided to do the same thing for the old farmhouse I was living in and it turned out well. Renovation is a good thing. God is making all things new. He lives here, the Bible says. He lives here among humans . . . and is renovating everything.

Sometimes it seems to me that we miss seeing the kind of things God is doing. Sometimes I think we probably get in the way of God's renovation projects or are not very open to them. Therefore it is a good thing for us to think about God's renovation program a little more. There are those in our acquaintance, even in the church, who readily agree that God has made a dwelling place with human beings. However, you can hardly tell that there is any renovation going on for them. I am not called by you or God to be anybody's judge, but it makes you wonder and it makes you worry. A passionate pastor wonders and worries about himself and his flock. On the other hand, the church is often filled with people in whose lives God's renovation projects are obvious all the time.

My father was without exception, and by a wide margin, the very best man I ever knew. As a consequence it is always very easy for me to believe that God is a God of absolutely unconditional grace. I saw it all the time in my father. I wish it had been as easy for my children to see that in me. However, what does it mean for us concretely that God lives here and is renovating everything? What should it mean to us as we look forward to the year ahead? What should it mean as we advance to the fall election as a nation? What should we look for and how should we conceive of that? It certainly seems like the text wants to speak very practically about God's renovation. The dwelling place of God is with humans. God lives here and God is making all things new. God has a grand and practical renovation project going for us as individuals, the church, and the world.

I suppose you could summarize this scripture in four words: love works, grace heals. That's what is going on. That is easy to say and difficult to describe. Therefore, it is often difficult to see. How can we join in and become part of God's project? How shall we get onboard? What does it look like operationally that God is renovating everything? What is God doing right now? What is God busy with as we speak? What does it look like in concrete terms? We need to figure out what that means and we need to talk about it operationally.

For twenty centuries the church has operated primarily theoretically. That is, we have done our theology in abstract theoretical categories and metaphors from ancient times and from an alien culture: the Hebrew Bible and old Israelite religion. I think that if we are to really appreciate and understand God's renovation project in this century, we need to start theologically from the bottom up and not from the top down. We must not articulate the Christian way from theory and theology, trying to work that down to some kind of operational meaningfulness. We have been doing that for two millennia. We have had some success at that, of course, but it seems to me that we have to start doing theology from the bottom up. I think in order to understand what it means that grace works and love heals, one has to start in the human condition. That is the condition of fear, neediness, loneliness, and dysfunction. We experience that condition personally in ourselves and we see it all around us, just as Jesus did.

It is interesting that Jesus did not start in a seminary. He did not start with theology. He did not write some books to explain what he was up to. He started down on the ground in human dysfunction and misery. He was not famous for being a great theologian or even a great preacher. He was famous for being a close intimate of whores and thieves, publicans and sinners. What does that mean? What does it mean to do the ministry of grace from that level? What does it mean to enact the operations of love pragmatically, starting where Jesus apparently started?

When God Moves In

It is interesting that the Pharisees knew very well how to speak of their approach, their system. They had a law-based system and so, operationally, it was easy enough to describe. We should give the Pharisees a great deal of credit. They were an admirable group of leaders. They really believed that if you wanted to renovate the people of God and this world you had to do it in a practical, operational way. The way to do it was to formulate a number of regulations to shape up human behavior. The Pharisees believed that if you translated obedience to those regulations into practical operational behavior, the outcome would be a world filled with people who were spiritually renewed.

Jesus' problem with that approach was that he did not believe you could do that. He did not believe that you could force obedient behavior and so cause a person's internal world to be renovated. Jesus was not altogether correct about that you know. The behaviorists, B.F. Skinner and others, demonstrated in the last century that there are certain things that you can accomplish in the change of human personality by constraining the external behavior. It is called *classical conditioning*. Part of my ministry to Kip, for example, was that I got him into a rehabilitation program for thirty days where he simply could not get any access to any drugs or alcohol. I had to constrain his behavior and the drier he got, the saner he got. The saner he got, the more his insides began to agree with what was better for him. It felt better to him to do right.

An alcoholic friend of mine once told me that one of the bad things about alcoholism is that when you get up in the morning feeling like death warmed over you realize that is the best you are going to feel all day. Good reason not to be there! So there are some limited things you can accomplish on the system of the Pharisees. Jesus' opposition to them was that he was sure you could not get spiritual renovation by external coercion. You cannot get a shift in the belief system if you start simply by constraining behavior and hoping it will internalize itself into a change of heart. A change of heart is necessary to the real change of life that God wants to bring about. That comes only from a new and deep illumination, a profoundly life-changing relationship, or an overwhelmingly meaningful accomplishment.

We have the Pharisee-types in our world today. They dominate the spiritual and religious scene. The reason why Al Qaeda destroyed the World Trade Center on September 11 is because they believe the Pharisees' system is correct. They believe that you should obey God, translate that into operational behavior, and then act that out. If you do you are justified by

God. Their belief in God is that anybody who is not a Muslim, a true deep devoted fundamentalist Muslim, is an infidel. They think that even other Arabs and Muslims who are not adequately intense about their Islamic faith are infidels and they must be converted or exterminated. They believed that punishing the United States of America by blowing down the towering symbol of American power and glory on September 11 would teach our country to change its ways.

What does it mean that God is renovating everything? Fundamentalism in any religion, whether Islamic, Christian, or Jewish, is a Pharisee kind of system. Having the right formulation of the creed, having the right theology, being able to say the name of God just right, and in that way being obedient to the formal structures of religion, is spiritual renewal. Translating that into behavior and feeling that you are justified before God is a dysfunctional notion of how God is renovating everything. We should be able to identify the operant factors that change lives in God's system of healing and redemption of human beings. What is it, operationally, to say that God is renovating everything? God is making all things new.

Today we know just about everything that needs to be known about how you change psychological and spiritual attitudes and behaviors. How shall we use that information about the way in which personalities change so that our inner selves get renovated and become more profoundly God's kind of self? Take, for example, the case of a woman who is getting her food out of garbage cans because her life has been destroyed by sexual abuse, drugs, divorce, loss, loneliness, and the inability to support herself. How will we operationally touch that person's neediness and bring the renovation that God wants brought there or that God is trying to work out for her? What will make the difference?

Well, one of the things we can do is to give her a place to sleep. We can give her a place to be safe. We can give her a place where she can be comfortable. We can make sure she is fed. We can do what I had to do with Kip: deprive her of access to the kinds of chemicals that are destructive for her. That lasts only as long as it lasts. How can we renovate her insides so that her outsides are also permanently renovated? That's what I mean by doing theology from the bottom up. You might call it theology from the inside out. How does one speak grace in that setting?

I do not think we can trust the theologians for that. They have too much invested in the theoretical perspective and its head-trip. They need to protect their world. We do need seminaries and we do need theology, but after the fact as descriptive, and not as the basic operation. World renovation is not going to come from the professionals. It is going to come from the people who understand what Ezekiel meant when he saw the Israelites in bondage in Babylon and he said, *I went there and I sat where they sat* (Ezek 3: 15). He put his arm around them in their place of need and misery and there he enacted the fact that love works and grace heals.

I once served a parish in which there was a lovely family with three little sons. They were good friends and so I had a nice relationship with the boys. The oldest boy was kind of timid and shy and when he would come out of the church and greeted me, I always joshed him around a bit and joked with him. One day his father came to me and he said, "You know, Dave is afraid of you." I thought, "Oh my God, afraid of me? How could he be afraid of me? I am always so friendly to him." He said "Afraid of you. You always speak loudly to him when he comes out of the church and you josh around with him and he is afraid of that."

The next Sunday when he came up the aisle I got down on my knees and I took his hand and I spoke quietly with him for a few minutes, gave him a hug and sent him on his way. It fixed it. He was not afraid. It shifted his insides. Something fundamental changed inside. I started there on the ground where he was. I sat where he sat. I felt the feelings that he felt and I responded to them. That is what this scripture means when it says, *God lives here. God has made his home with us.*

Everything that the gospels tell us says plainly that God has entered into our world. God lives here, and by living here and acting out the fact that love heals and grace works, God renovates the whole world. God is renovating us and the entire world! God is busy remodeling. Paul took that so seriously that he said the whole world is standing on tip-toe waiting for the time when this renovation comes to its completion. It is waiting for the full manifestation of the people of God. It is waiting to hear the loud announcement, *God has made his home with us and has made it clear, God is renovating everything . . . making all things new, from the bottom up.*

What do you think that will look like? Will it look like the rushing mighty wind of God's Pentecost Spirit blowing once more through the church and the world? Will it empowers us with the Pentecost flame of fire so that the spirituality of every heart flames up brightly? Can you receive that? What will that do for your life? Will that empower us to change the institutions and structures and powers of this world that devalue and denigrate or neglect humankind?

By Grace Alone

The wind of the Spirit is blowing and God continues the renovation project that will continue to change people and the world. Let us keep an eye open for how the Spirit shows up around the next corner so we may discern exactly our operational role in God's project. We want to be on the right side of this renovation program, I am sure—not part of the problem but part of the solution.

Amen. So let it Be!

SERMON THIRTEEN

The Purposes of Prayer
—Matthew 6:1–13

> Do not pray like hypocrites and pagans.
> — MATTHEW 6:5A

> Your Father knows what you need before you ask.
> — MATTHEW 6:8

I SUPPOSE EVERY HUMAN being is interested in the theme, *The Purposes of Prayer*. Everyone wonders about the nature, purpose, function, and outcome of prayer. Prayer is a mystery at best, even to those of us who have lived a life of prayer for three fourths of a century.

I have a family of friends whose third daughter was born with hydrocephalus. They were shocked and very anxious. So they did what godly people do. They prayed for the child. Indeed, they laid their hands upon the child's head and prayed for her to be a normal child. Within days the hydrocephalus receded and Linda is a wonderfully normal person, bright, healthy, and godly. She is herself a woman with a profoundly prayerful life. Physicians tell me that sometimes hydrocephalus spontaneously cures itself. However that may be, they prayed and Linda was healed. What counts for that family and for me is just that. That is as real as the sunshine in the morning.

My father prayed regularly for rain in times of drought, or for the rain to stop and the sun to shine when the fields were too wet to work. He prayed for my brother's healing from pneumonia. He prayed for my brother when we thought he had been killed in a hay-baler accident. His prayers were answered. Those two brothers are alive and in their eighties. We were not wealthy in the Great Depression and we lost our corn crop and the second cutting of hay to the hot dry sun in 1937, but we managed and lived well enough for that time and setting. I remember that year less as a time of distress and more as a time when our family spent a lot of time in prayer.

We had a neighbor who was disillusioned with the church, with faith, with prayer, and with God. He thought my father was rather naïve in his life of devotion and prayer. He was quite sure that when the drought came or when the climate was congenial, it was simply the natural cyclical process of nature. Its effect on us was an accident of history and the chance one took at this crap shoot called life. He was not an unhappy man. I really kind of liked his jovial and devil-may-care outlook on life. He told unbelievably good jokes.

However, there was a difference in my father's outlook on life and that of our neighbor that I found deep, mysterious, and reassuring. The family that prayed for their daughter knew that when Linda was healed it was of God—a gift of grace. My father knew that when the rain came in the late fall of 1937 and the winter wheat flourished so we had a good crop in the spring that it was a gift of God's goodness to us. We knew that when the year was prosperous it was not an accident of history but a providence motivated by God's grace. Our neighbor was sure it was the luck of the draw. What really interested me was the difference in the quality of life that those two different ways of looking at things produced. The prayer perspective always seemed quite mysterious to me but the difference it made in the quality of our life seemed to me to make a life of prayer more than worthwhile.

The Bible says that Jesus prayed a lot. He is reported to have gone away by himself frequently to some isolated place and to have spent the entire night in prayer. It is, therefore, interesting that Jesus seemed to have a great deal of resistance to public and communal prayer. His disciples wanted him

The Purposes of Prayer

to teach them to pray but apparently he was disinclined to do so. The story in Matthew's gospel that is our scripture for today is very interesting in that regard. It seems that the disciples had been taking this matter up with Jesus for some time and he refused to give them a formula for their prayers. At least in our story for today they seem to be coming to him with a certain sense of desperation, since they finally confront him with an argument that he just cannot get around. They tell him that John the Baptist teaches his disciples to pray so why does Jesus not do so.

Remember that two of John's former disciples followed Jesus. Do we hear a little blackmail here? Is there a suggestion in their argument that they might very well return to John and leave Jesus? In Mark 8:29–32 the multitudes have forsaken Jesus and he asks whether the disciples will also abandon him. Obviously the disciples feel that they have some leverage for their request by citing the case of John. They were quite obviously reminding him that if they could not get what they want from him they could seek it from John.

So in Matthew's story, Jesus relents and decides to teach them to pray. It is interesting how he introduces that teaching regarding prayer. He starts out by saying something like, *Well, if you must have a formula for prayer, then pray as follows.* However, he then tells them some ways of praying that they should assiduously avoid. *Do not pray like hypocrites who stand on street corners and pray publicly so that they may be seen and praised by the crowds. That would be praying like the Pharisee in the temple in the parable of the Pharisee and Publican.* He declares that people who pray like that only want their prayers to bring them public esteem, and it does do that much at least. So their prayers are answered, not by God but by the crowd's response.

Then he commands his disciples not to pray like the pagans who pray endless and obsessively verbose prayers, haranguing God with a superfluity of verbiage, sometimes called *logorrhea*, like verbal (*logos*) diarrhea. *Do not pray like that,* Jesus counseled. You will remember that the prophets of Baal on Mt. Carmel with Elijah prayed like that and were not heard. Such efforts to attract God's attention by compulsively spinning a prayer wheel, dancing as a whirling dervish, rocking back and forth at the Wailing Wall, or obsessively reciting a traditional ritual would seem to be useless and inappropriate, according to Jesus. Indeed, such behaviors imply that God is someone who can be manipulated by such methods.

Moreover, Jesus said that the disciples, if they really insisted on praying at all, should not think that they can manipulate God in any way. He said it is inappropriate to try to talk God into doing nice things for you that God would not have the good sense or presence of mind to do if you did not talk God into it. Jesus assured them that God knows what we need before we ask. Moreover God is always busy giving us everything we need, so far as it is possible and good for us.

Jesus clearly thought that people should pray as a secret communion with God directly, letting the spirit effervesce, as it were, in the presence of God. Prayer may be more a matter of reflective consciousness than implorations. Jesus seemed to think it was mostly a matter of thanksgiving and celebration of God than presenting petitions. An old hymn says:

> Prayer is the soul's sincere *desire, Unuttered* or expressed,
> A *motion* of a *hidden fire*, That trembles in the breast.
> Prayer is the *burden* of a *sigh*, The *falling* of a tear,
> The *upward glancing* of the eye, When only God is near.
> Prayer is the Christians *vital breath*, The Christians *native air*,
> Our watchword at the gate of death. We enter heaven with prayer.
>
> (James Montgomery, Prayer is the Soul's Sincere Desire, 1818)

Jesus urged us that when we pray we should enter into a closet, close the door, and pray to God in secret, confident that God who hears in secret will answer our prayers.

Jesus really seemed to be implying that prayer was not really necessary and that a lot of types of prayer were really lousy ways of trying to express our spirituality or relationship with God. He implied that living a life of conscious trust and responsibility before the face of God was the real thing. It was clear from his approach that God-consciousness was very good and God-manipulation was dumb and useless. In fact, Jesus said about everything one needs to say to argue that petitionary prayer is really unnecessary at best. At worst it is a failure to trust God's continual grace and providence to us, giving the impression that we must beg God for it.

What is surprising is that after his firm cautionary introduction he did finally teach the disciples a prayer and in it there are *four petitions*. Now why did he do that? He gave us the Lord's Prayer (Matt 6:9–12). It has three sections. The first one extols God and asserts that we know God is in charge and we know that it is a good thing for us that God is in charge. We are for that and we wish to align ourselves with that reality. "Our father who art in heaven, hallowed be thy name. Thy kingdom come, they will be done, on earth as it is in heaven." That is like saying, "Oh God, we are for what you are for and we gladly give ourselves to it."

The third section is a doxology, that is, a song of praise. "Yours is the kingdom, the power, and the glory, forever." That was the sentence with which most Jewish prayers had been concluded for centuries. When we pray those words we mean to affirm that we are those who stand in awe of the majesty and magnificence of all we experience of God in nature and in grace. Those words are a way of saying that we are so very glad that God is God and grace is grace.

It is the center section of the prayer that is troublesome or mystifying in view of what Jesus said at the outset. Here are four petitions: "Give us this day our daily bread. Forgive us our trespasses just as we forgive our trespassers. Bring us not into temptation. Deliver us from evil." Why would Jesus build this prayer around four such fundamental petitions when he had just explained so forcefully that petitionary prayer was unnecessary and probably an offensive act of unfaithfulness before the face of God who already knows and provides what we need before we ask God?

This much we know: Jesus did not give us these four fundamental petitions about daily food, forgiveness, protection, and deliverance because he thought God would not give us these graces unless we talked God into doing so. Jesus had just assured us that such could never be the case. "God knows what you need before you ask." So there must be another reason. If petitions in prayer are not designed to persuade God who are they for? Well they must then be for us. If they do not manipulate or influence God they must influence us in some necessary way.

My brother in law, Edson T. Lewis, is a minister in Columbus, Ohio. A couple of years ago I asked him to write a chapter in a book I was publishing called *Psychology and the Bible*. He wrote a long and sturdy chapter on spirituality, arguing that spirituality is a matter of our posture toward God. That is, spirituality has to do with how we stand toward God. He reminded us of his experience with his seven year old grandson who was taking karate, and whose success in it depended upon the posture he was able to hold toward the instructor or toward any opponent. Effectiveness in the relationship, friend or foe, depended upon and was a matter of posture.

Lewis explained that he thought spirituality, our relationship with God, was also a matter of posture. It depends upon how we stand toward God, with regard to God. Jesus seems to have understood that. So he gave us the four petitions, not to talk God into doing nice or necessary things for us that God would not otherwise have had the presence of mind or good sense to do. He gave us those four petitions so that on the fundamental matters of our existence we would stand toward God as needy children lifting up our hands and hearts to God, and making it plain that we understand how we depend upon God's good providence and grace.

The petitions are for us, to create a proper posture toward God. They are not for God, who does not need them in order to remember what we need and desire to fill our needs. They are for us so that we will continue to cultivate in our inner selves that sense of living and moving and having our being from God's hands of grace, mercy, and love. These four petitions, and all of our crying out to God in our neediness throughout life, are for the cultivation of our sense of being God's people who await God's kind largess.

That is what was happening in my father, and in our family, and not in our neighbor. We knew who we were. We were God's needy children; and it felt good to us to be that. We were glad and we prayed the first and last sections of the Lord's Prayer with joy and trust and celebration, because the middle section kept us properly oriented. When the rain fell on us and on our neighbor, we knew it was a gift to us from our heavenly father and that made all the difference in the world as to how we felt about it. Our friend down the road was glad for the rain which he considered just a lucky turn in the weather. We weathered the drought in the sure knowledge that the thin thread upon which life is suspended was firmly held on the other end by our provident God. That was our posture. It made all the difference in the world!

So, in the end, prayer is a great—a heavenly—mystery. Who can explain it? Who can account for it all? It blessed Linda's life with wholeness and wholesomeness. It healed her. It got us through the Great Depression and the War as humble, secure, and grateful people. It blessed us. I do not know that our outer world would have been any different had we not been a praying family. I know that without it our inner world would have been barren and empty.

I am sure I have not exploded all the mysteries of prayer for you. I think it would be unfortunate if I did. The only way to find out about prayer is to do it, to experiment with it, to explore it deeply. Samuel Taylor Coleridge said wisely, "More things are wrought by prayer than this world dreams of." Amen. So let it Be!

SERMON FOURTEEN

Do You Fear God?
— Mark 1:1-4, 1:14-15, 1:21-28

> The fear of the Lord is the beginning of wisdom.
> —Psalm 111:10

Do you fear God? The Bible says, "The fear of the Lord is the beginning of wisdom. A good understanding have all those who practice it. The praise of God endures forever" (Ps. 111:10). The Psalmist's claim is enigmatic. It brings together in one breath fear of God and praise of God.

One of the interesting things about human life and history is the fact that everywhere, all the time, everybody is religious. You could say that human beings are spontaneously and universally God-fearing. God created us in such a way that we have a deep inner spiritual quality. We did not ask for it, just as we did not ask for a beating heart or a thinking brain. It is inherent to our nature. The special spiritual quality in us is that deep inner mystical part that hungers always for the meaning of things.

That is, our spirituality is irrepressible and universal. It is something like the Spirit of God that pervades the whole world. The Bible suggests that God's spirituality prompted God so much to love the world that God created the world. What a great adventure for God to set in motion this grand evolutionary process of the unfolding of life and history; God trying to find out the meaning of everything and how it can work out over time. Our spirituality is like that. It is that inner spiritual quality in us all, hungering and thirsting for the meaning of everything in time and eternity, that makes human beings universally religious—universally God-fearing.

The difficulty lies in the fact that trying to figure out what it means to be religious, appropriately and healthily, is fairly complicated. For most people, most of the time, most everywhere being a God-fearing person means to be scared of God. So I ask you, do you fear God? In what way is that true of you?

When we are children we are always uncomfortable because there is so much of life that is unknown. Many of us never get over this sense of the unknown and the anxiety about it. In some ways it becomes a larger problem as we mature. The more we learn the more we realize how vast the unknown really is. There is so much that is out of our control, so much beyond us. There is so much about life that we have to learn and that we have to do. Every task and every challenge seems to stretch us a little more. That is good, of course, but it also makes us feel both inadequate and uncomfortable. I find that sometimes it is genuinely painful. Psychologists tell us that the inevitable consequence of that childhood quest is that we always end up feeling that we never quite measure up. We are usually not clear on what it is that we do not measure up to. Nonetheless we feel like we are falling short of the mark.

It may be that we fall short of what our parents expect or of what we think our parents expect. We may fall short of what we think they should expect of us. We may feel that we fall short of what we think God expects or of what God really does expect. Thus it may come down to the values we have internalized from God or from others, as we understood them. We may, of course, fall short of our own idealized standards. We may feel that we do not quite know how to measure up, that our database is inadequate to the responsibilities of life and the challenges of godliness. That is always true to some extent, of course. It is not only true of us as children but it is true of us all throughout our lives.

However, psychologists tell us that as children we tend to internalize this discomfort as guilt and shame. We think, "There must be something wrong with me because I feel uncomfortable about the fact that I do not quite measure up. I did not understand what mother said or required of me. I did not do it quite right. She handled it pretty well, but nonetheless, I realized in myself that I fell short. I feel guilty and I feel shame." Maybe I thought Mother and Father, or God, expected more of me than they really did, so my own imagination is the measure or standard of how I fall short. I fall short of my own expectations, and I internalize that as guilt and shame.

So you can see how, as we go on in life, we project this sense of guilt and shame upon God. Thus we develop our sense of threat concerning what are God's expectations of us. In that sense, everybody fears God, but what does it mean to be God-fearing in the sense of which the Psalmist speaks? For most people, unfortunately, it means that there is much about God and what God expects of us that is unknown. That is enough to make us perpetually fearful that we may not understand God's expectations adequately or measure up properly.

So we carry ourselves with a sense of God being a bit of a threat, or perhaps even a very great threat. We may say to ourselves, "Just in case I did not quite measure up, or just in case I did not quite understand, I better watch out!" So all the while we reflect upon that in that way. The backdrop is our awareness that we lack adequate knowledge about God. That generates great concern about how that affects our ultimate destiny. Out of that enigma has come all the crazy notions of eternal punishment, hell, and so forth—all erroneous fictions.

The point is that human finitude makes us feel inadequate. Our inadequacy gives us the inherent sense that we fall short and that we may, therefore, be under some kind of threat somehow, even if we do not know what kind of threat it is. I think that even atheists work so hard at claiming that God does not exist because that is a way of creating a world view that is essentially one of denial. They are busy trying to rule God out of the equation because they are quite sure that if God is within the equation, God is dangerous. "So let us see if we can get rid of God," they say.

Some people need to have a divine threat and a well-populated hell in order to anchor their world view. They have sold out to the notion that God is a cosmic threat. Yesterday I had a young lady in my office whose mother is a Chinese Buddhist and her father is a professor at a university in England. He derives from Christian tradition but is basically a secular person. I spoke with her about her life, values, hopes for the future, and how I could help her.

At that point she felt it appropriate to the conversation to tell me that she was an unbeliever. I asked her what she meant by that and she said, "I cannot believe that there is any sense to the notion that God is dangerous and that he has a hell waiting for us, and that if we cannot figure out how to behave ourselves appropriately our destiny is hopeless." She said to me, "I think that such a kind of God is not believable."

I said to her, "You are right. Such a kind of God is not only absurd, but is a monster! Nobody ought to believe in such a kind of God." She discerned that whatever was true of God, he ought at least to be as decent a person as you and I ascribe to be, attempt to be, and desire to be. If we can figure out what our best nature could possibly be and work for it, God ought to be at least a little better than that.

"If I can be forgiving and kind, tender and gentle, decent and loving, and God cannot, God is a monster; and I do not believe in such a God. I do not want him." Basically, that was the thrust of her conversation. It was brilliant for a sixteen-year-old, and it took great courage to say that out loud.

All religions throughout history and throughout the world have been built around the basic notion that God is a threat. All the sacrificial systems, all the human and animal sacrifices, all the child sacrifice, and all the horrid things done throughout history under the name of Christianity, and every other kind of religion, comes out of this central fact that God is a threat and God needs to be placated somehow. We have to do something for God that helps him get his head screwed back on right, so that he can be as decent to us as good humans are to each other.

The notion that God is a warrior God of violent danger to humans comes out of an idea embedded deeply in early Israelite religion, narrated for us in the ancient documents of the Hebrew Bible. It has been seeded into all three of the Abrahamic religions: Judaism, Christianity, and Islam. It is the notion that in this world we are up against a cosmic conflict and God is up against it too. God is up against a counter god, an evil god, and we better make sure we are on the right side in this contest, the outcome of which is not yet clear.

That notion of a cosmic conflict is not true, of course. There is no evidence for it in human experience. There is no basis for it even in the Bible, properly understood. Those parts of the Bible which make a case for a cosmic conflict do not ring true to the Bible's mainstream message of God's unconditional and universal grace. The grand exception, in all of human history, to this notion of God as a threat, caught up in a cosmic conflict, is the illumination experienced by Abraham in Genesis 12 and 17.

Do You Fear God?

Akhenaton, the monotheistic Egyptian pharaoh may also have sensed the same reality of God's forgiving grace.

Abraham's notion of God was that of God declaring, *I will be a God to you and to your children after you throughout their generations, for an everlasting covenant, no strings attached. You will be my people and I will be your God.* That is the only exception, in all of world religions, to the general fact that God is universally seen as a threat. Abraham's great breakthrough vision was the notion that God could be a God who steps beyond our human inadequacy and our sin,, reaches around behind all of our inadequacy and self-justification, and embraces us in God's fundamental goodwill, in spite of these things. That is a unique vision of God as a God of unconditional and universal grace and acceptance of us. That is the remarkable Jewish tradition that came to flower in Jesus Christ.

Unfortunately, of course, it took only a thousand years after Abraham for the Israelites to lose their grip on this good news of God's grace and turn Israelite religion into a religion of divine threat and human placation of that threat. When Jesus cut back through all the accretions of paganism that overlay the Israelite religion of his time, he took us back to the God of grace. Then it took the Christian Church only five hundred years to revert to conditional and legalistic theology. When Martin Luther restored the gospel of grace to the front and center of the church's consciousness again in the sixteenth century, it took the Protestants only 250 years to revert to scholastic corruption of the clear clarion call of the gospel of unconditional grace. We are getting more efficient in achieving utter paganism in our theological systems. That is a result of the instinctual fear that God is a threat.

The only way the ancient Israelites seemed able to explain that their failed national and international policy resulted in domestic turmoil and corruption, as well as in international conflict and exile from their own land, was by concluding that God was punishing them. God, the warrior, had exercised divine authority and power to do them in for their human perfidy. Whenever that God has a major problem he resorts immediately to ultimate violence to punish the one who caused God's discomfort. That God is a monster no one should worship.

There was one bright moment in Egyptian history in the life of Akhenaton. He broke with the Egyptian priests and established monotheism as the official religion. Barbara Mertz wrote a lovely book called, *Red Land, Black Land* (Delta, 1988), in which she described Egyptian civilization. After describing all the amazing things found in Egyptian tombs relating to their contemplation of the afterlife, including especially the very complex and elaborate funerary arrangements that the Egyptians employed, she made a point of the fact that what we can see here is their struggle to come to terms with this notion of God as a threat.

On the one hand they were rather afraid that God was dangerous. They had lots of reasons for thinking this way, including the reasons the Israelites had formulated, namely, that God would justifiably punish their failures. On the other hand, however, Akhenaton expressed in a poetic prayer on the wall of his tomb a theology of God as capable of forgiving grace. The poem is almost like one of the psalms in our Bible. There he says, "Oh God, if it is possible that you could deal with me, not in terms of your justice, but in your mercy . . . ." A bright moment of insight!

Like the sixteen year old girl in my office, this pharaoh saw beyond the monster God of threat, the possibility that filled Abraham's soul. Abraham saw and Akhenaton hoped that God can embrace us as dear and beloved children in spite of ourselves. Barbara Mertz said that we ought to look at all the funerary complexity of Egyptian culture and discern the Egyptian's attempt to deal with "our common human terror and our common hope" (367). Those words move me profoundly. They are the final line of her wonderful book.

The great tragedy is that for twenty centuries Christianity has been more a religion of God-threat than of God's grace. Jesus preached good news. It was even more than John the Baptist's good news of *salvation by means of repentance*. Jesus' gospel was simply a call to open-hearted embrace of the good news of *unconditional acceptance* by God. Jesus knew that many of our reasons for falling short of the mark are not even known to ourselves, so how could we repent of them. God's grace is greater than all our failures and flaws. The good news is that God can embrace us in grace even if we cannot figure out how to repent, or for what to repent.

It seems, however, that it never takes us long, after our vision of the profound grace of God, to fall back into the mindset of fear of God as threat. So even Christians have tended to fear God in a wrong-headed and sick way! From this has come all of the New Age Ideology that we see everywhere now. Without being able to figure out how to counter the religion of divine threat, young people have begun to surmise on their own that there must be a better way, a more sensible way, a healthier way to look at this whole matter. So they have tried to paste together some aspects of various traditions: Eastern, Christian, and primitive religions. Out of it they have manufactured the completely fictional myth that is called New Age Theology. It is simply an attempt to escape from the God of threat.

So I need to ask you whether you fear God. The Psalm says everybody should. Why would the Bible say that you should, in the light of the good news of unconditional grace in Jesus and Paul? Well, it is because the King James Version of the Bible translated that word from Hebrew into an English word which no longer means what the Hebrew word intends. We have been stuck with it ever since 1611 CE. The Bible does not intend to say that we should be fearful of God in the sense of God being a threat. The Bible, if we know how to read the theme of grace throughout it, says that God is not a threat—absolutely not a threat to anyone, even the most evil person.

We should never have even a smidgen of concern about God being dangerous to us or anyone. That Hebrew word in Psalm 111:10 means awe, to stand in awe of God. That is why the next line of the psalm emphasizes that we should praise God. We are called to stand in awe of God's greatness in creation and in God's providence, and to praise God for God's goodness and grace. That is what the psalm intends and the godly posture to which it calls us. *Standing in awe of the Lord is the beginning of wisdom. It is the only way to get the truth and meaning of everything straight. All those who stand in awe of God have a good understanding.* That is why the psalm can close by saying "His praise endures forever" (Psalm 111:10).

We come here on Sunday morning to worship and praise God. That is what this verse is about. It is not about perceiving God as a threat, a God focused on shaping us up. It is about standing in awe of God, living life with this wonderfully free sense of the awesomeness of God, the wonder of God. God is not in the business of shaping us up but of cheering us up with God's good news of unconditional forgiveness for everybody for everything for evermore.

Christianity is not a threat by which to be shaped up. It is not a command to be obeyed. It is not a burden to be labored under. It is not an ordeal to be endured. It is not a danger to be avoided, negotiated, or placated. Christianity is the spirituality of forgiving grace: a freedom to be exploited, an invitation to be seized and celebrated, a sense of peace beyond human comprehension. The reason to be a Christian is because it is more fun—living in the freedom and relief of God's sure and complete forgiveness.

We are invited to live life out of that sense of things. In that context we can understand Paul in Romans 8:38: "I am persuaded that neither death nor life; nor powers from on high, nor powers on earth, nor powers from below; nor things past, present or future; nor any agents from heaven or hell, nor anything else in all God's creation shall ever be able to separate us from the love of God that is in Christ Jesus, our Lord."

Amen. So let it Be!

SERMON FIFTEEN

Is Jesus Really God?
—John 1:1–14; Mark 15:34–39

> In the beginning was the Logos . . . and the Logos became human and lived with us.
>
> — JOHN 1:1, 1:14

> Surely this man was a Son of God.
>
> — LUKE 23:47; MATTHEW 27:54B

IT IS NOT SURPRISING that people want to hear sermons on the question of whether Jesus is really God. Of course, I could honestly answer the question with a simple, "Yes!" and then we could all go home. However, I gather that you realize the issue is somewhat more complicated than that. Furthermore, this is the central question in Christian theology. It is always worth revisiting. This topic can and must be approached from many perspectives because a sound and satisfying answer to it is both exceedingly important and infinitely complex. I shall try to get at that complexity along the following pathways. I will approach the question in terms of the problem of language—the meaning of the words we use about God. Then I will set forth the various things the Bible says about it. After that I will describe the church's historic struggle with giving an answer to that central question. Finally, I will say what can be said about interpreting that question and its answer in twenty-first century meanings.

First, then, let me say a few words about the problem of God-language. All of us talk about God rather freely. That is as it should be. However, if I asked you to draw a picture of God or describe what you mean or envision when you speak of God, you would find that task difficult. It is difficult to concretely depict God and each of you would have a different and highly personal notion to express. We can say a lot of concrete things about what God does. God created the world. God visited us in the person of Jesus. God calls us to be responsible and godly people. God shows up in our experience in the intimations and illuminations of the guiding Spirit. That, however, is quite a different thing from saying anything about who God is or what God is like.

We only know what God's behavior is like, and most of that is what we have learned from what others have said about what we can count on from God. I say to you often that I believe that God is a God of unconditional grace. That is my claim regarding God and I make it because I believe the Bible backs that up solidly. However, the Bible is the testimony of other people like me who made this claim on the basis of what they thought was their experience, illumined by the Divine Spirit.

That means that when we talk about Jesus being God it is very difficult to say what that sentence means. We can easily say that Jesus acted in the way we expect God to act: kind, loving, generous, challenging, insistent upon justice and decency, and full of grace. However, that is not the same as being able to say that Jesus is God. We do not know what God is and what it would be like for a man to be God or a piece of God. When we speak of God we can only speak in human metaphors or word-pictures. Even when we say that God is the creator, we are using a term that describes a human characteristic, and we are metaphorically applying it to God.

We may be completely off-base with our anthropomorphic metaphors. When we say that God is a creator, we mean God is a person who thought out how to fashion the material world and then decided by an act of will to make what God had designed. Perhaps God is not a creator. Perhaps God is not a person, who exists outside this world and who created this material

Is Jesus Really God?

world out there, outside of God's self. All these terms, person, creator, him, grace, and love are words which describe human characteristics, and we project them onto God as descriptive of God. We do this because we do not have any other language with which to talk about God, other than these human metaphors.

It is possible that instead of being a person out there somewhere outside of the material world, who thought up the idea of how a material world should be and then decided to fashion it, God is really a massive, generative, grace-filled force out of whom the material world emerged, or oozed out just because God is that kind of a generative force. Perhaps God's nature, wisdom, creativity, imagination, and generative capabilities are infinitely greater than anything we can capture in such human-like terms or characteristics as our simple words for creator, person, father, spirit, him, her, grace, love. It is possible that God exists as an entity of an order of magnitude and magnificent majesty far beyond anything that the word *person* could possibly express.

Those words do not define God. They only describe in a frail human way how we experience God's existence impacting ours. Friedrich Schleiermacher, a great preacher and man of God, was sure that God was the life force which permeates the entire material universe and makes it vital and generative, physically and spiritually. Baruch Spinoza, a Christian philosopher, held a similar perspective and thought that the material world is the body of God in which the life force is God's spirit or the divine soul alive in everything that lives. They may be right. I am inclined to be such a panentheist.

So when we ask, "Is Jesus really God?" it is difficult to know if we can possibly understand what we are asking, to say nothing about discerning what could possibly be an answer to that question. However, let us look to the Bible to see whether it has a useful answer. We must depend mainly on the New Testament to help us, since that is the sacred scripture that tells us the story of Jesus' life and its meaning. The comments of the first three gospels upon this question can be summarized quite easily. Mark, Matthew, and Luke describe Jesus as a man born of Mary, who felt urgently moved by God as Spirit to preach about the fact that God's reign of grace and love was about to flourish on this planet within two generations.

He said that the reign of God's grace and love was already evident wherever human beings took care of each other, motivated by their reverence for God. Those first three gospels complete their story by describing

Jesus as a righteous man who was exalted by God to heavenly status after his catastrophic death at the hands of those who opposed God's coming reign of grace and love. Matthew, Mark, and Luke promise that this exalted Jesus would return in twenty to forty years, with the power and glory of God, to exterminate those who oppose God's reign and to bring fully into existence that divine rule of grace that works and love that heals.

Thus, in our text for today, the centurion declares in Matthew's gospel that Jesus was surely a son of God. That would seem to answer our question, except that "a son of God" in that day meant a righteous or innocent man, as we have the centurion's words in Luke. Thus Paul refers to all of us as sons of God, since we have been unconditionally forgiven in God's grace and God has imputed righteousness to us. Moreover, whenever Jesus refers to God in the first three gospels, he always speaks as though God is somebody else: his father, our father, the one to whom we go when we die, the one who is imposing the awful ordeal upon him in Gethsemane, and the one who abandoned him on the cross. Those gospels do not describe Jesus in a manner like the Apostles' Creed tries to speak of him, defining him as God.

However, the Gospel of John, as well as Paul in Philippians 2, Colossians 1, and Romans 8 specifically say that Jesus is divine. John says that the spirit or essential nature of God came down from God into this world and took up residence in a man from Nazareth named Jesus. This person was a son of God whose uniqueness was in the fact that he was the Son of Man (John 3:13–18, 5:27–47). The Son of Man in Jewish tradition was a heavenly figure whom John says descended from heaven and later ascended again to heaven, returning to his original divine glory and proper residence (John 3:13–14). John's gospel makes clear that he will not return again to earth but is always present on earth as the Divine Spirit (John 14). The purpose of the Divine Spirit's descent to earth to take up residence in Jesus was to reveal to all of us the mysteries of God as a God of grace and love, and to save all humans (John 3:16–17). Paul says that in Jesus, filled as he was with the Divine Spirit, the full godhead was present in material form (Col 1:15–20).

Now that idea seems to answer our question, *Is Jesus really God*? However, what do John and Paul mean? Do they mean that the man from Nazareth was *a man with a life full of God,* as Marcus Borg declares (lecture, First Presbyterian Church of Northville, Northville, MI, Jan 23, 1997)? Do they mean that there is a third kind of being having some kind of nature between

Is Jesus Really God?

a divine being in heaven and human beings on earth. That seems to be the picture as described by John and Paul, though not by the first three gospels? If they mean such an identity of being, is that different from the way in which *we* are persons with a life full of God, or identified in *being* with God? We are, after all, God's image-bearers and God's heartily believing people. The issue is complex. When speaking of God we are always speaking in human word-pictures and never quite sure exactly what we mean by them.

The church tried to solve the problem and give a definitive answer, once and for all. The community of believers began immediately after Jesus' death to try to answer that question, *Is Jesus really God*? For the first three centuries they could not come to any agreement on the question, and by 300 CE there were almost as many different answers to our question as there were Christian believers. They fought over the issue, condemned each other to hell over the issue, killed each other over this question, and in the end never agreed. Some of their answers to the question were fantastic, such as those of the Gnostics Christians.

Finally, Constantine forced them to get together on the answer. So the bishops formulated the Apostles' Creed, the Nicene Creed, the Athanasian Creed, and some other creeds, to try to get a final unified answer. They tried to define God. Then they tried to define Jesus as God. The trouble was that the Bible spoke only in metaphors about this question and about the nature of Jesus. When the bishops tried to formulate definitions of God and Jesus for the creeds from 325 CE to 451 CE, they thought they could translate those Hebrew metaphors from the Bible into Greek philosophical definitions.

The Old Testament and New Testament had always talked about God in terms of the way we experience God affecting our lives. In the fourth and fifth century the Greek Christians wanted to define divine being in abstract philosophical terms and categories. It did not work. Read all those ancient creeds and notice that they all have different ways of expressing their attempt to answer our basic question, and none of them really answers it. They just give us a lot of philosophical terms that are no better than the ancient biblical metaphors were at tying down the precise meaning of the being of God, and the being of God in Christ. So many words, so little certain meaning! A muffled trumpet at best!

So what shall we do with all this today? How can we interpret the question and its answer in the twenty-first century? Is Jesus really God?

By Grace Alone

Let me say the following about it. First, it is not altogether clear why this is such a crucial question. What difference does it make for us if Jesus of Nazareth was a man in whom God's spirit was remarkably present to us, as it can be in you or me; or if Jesus was God's being visiting us in the form of a real man? Second, we know he was a real man, born in the flesh. We know the centurion was right, that he was God's ideal man, empowered by the Divine Spirit. The record of his life is plain enough in that regard. Third, if Jesus was God's being visiting us in the form of a real man, how should we describe that phenomenon differently than saying "Truly this man was a son of God," meaning that he was a righteous man, God's kind of man, God's man, the God-man, a man with a life full of God?

Fourth, this much we know: God was, in Jesus Christ, reconciling the world unto God's self. We know that because we have all experienced that reconciliation and the assurance that comes with it. Moreover, we know that God sent Jesus into the world not to condemn the world but that the world through him should be saved (Jn 3:15–17). We know that whosoever believes in him as God present to us is already saved, namely, already living the relieved life of God's unconditional forgiveness and acceptance—life on God's plane of existence.

Of course, every word in that last paragraph is a metaphor in which we have tried to catch a transcendent meaning. That is never wholly possible; but then do we really need more than our metaphors? Do we really need a definition of the very being, essence, and ontology of God? Do we really need a definition of the very being of Jesus to feel safe or satisfied? Do we need a Jesus with a life fuller of God than yours and mine is *intended* by God to be?

We know that God is present to us in Jesus of Nazareth, because holding to his commission and command works; and he has made us into the people of God, the people in whom grace works and love heals. We experience the intimations of Jesus' Spirit. It does not get any better than that! Nor do we need any more than that. God is in Christ embracing us to God's self.

Amen. So let it Be!

SERMON SIXTEEN

For God's Pleasure and Purpose

—Psalm 149:1–6a; Numbers 6:24–26

GOD TAKES PLEASURE IN the people of God. So may God bless you and keep you. May you experience God's shining smile turned toward you. May God be gracious to you! May God's radiant joy in you be clear to you. May God give you a deep sense of peace and prosperity.

The entire Bible conspires to commnicate the message that our fear, guilt, and shame have been erased from God's way with us. Since that is true, what is the motivation to keep on working hard at being God's kind of person? Since we cannot sin ourselves out of God's grace what is the sustaining driver behind our trying to attain quality values and idealism? Since God has guaranteed to every human being God's unconditional forgiveness and acceptance of us as we are, no strings attached, why consider God at all? If grace is universal, in spite of whether we are good, bad, or indifferent, why not just cut our own swath in life as we please and stop worrying about trying to be God's kind of people? Since Hitler, Stalin, Genghis Khan, Osama bin Laden, and the genocidal Israeli who exterminated the Canaanites in 1200 BCE are going to be in heaven, why should I not be an arrogant and narcissistic corporate executive who lives by greed and manipulation? If there is not a well-populated hell, give me a good reason to be a Christian.

"God takes pleasure in God's people. God adorns the humble hearted with triumphant prosperity" (Ps 149:4). None of us owns the past. It is gone and there is nothing we can do about that. God owns the past and God can handle it. God spends much of the time cleaning it up so that it is pristinely pure in God's view. Everybody's past looks saintly to God after the good housecleaning of divine grace. We do not even know very much about the present. We experience the fact that some of the things we do in the present affect our lives positively or negatively. We get the impression that we have some influence upon the present. We also have reason to believe that if we do some good things with the present, that we have somewhat in hand, that gives us a chance at a useable future. God is glad to take charge of our past and clean it up thoroughly and at the same time offer us the present for our use and development. God takes pleasure in what God's people do with the present so that we have some kind of quality future.

The reason God takes possession of our past is so that we do not continue to hang on to the fear, guilt, and shame that we have about it. Freed from those by God's grace we are completely free to do whatever we wish with the present. We merely need to accept the effects our use of the present has upon our future. However, even then when our present becomes our past God owns it and cleans it up again. What a deal we have! The gift of freedom from psychic and spiritual wasted energy! We are free to use all that freed up energy for growing in wisdom and knowledge about God and the godly way for us into our future. What a deal grace really is!

How do you feel about having a guaranteed pleasurable future? For the next moment and for ever? Perhaps I need to ask a prior question. Do you believe that you cannot sin yourself out of God's grace or squirm out of God's long embrace? Are you honestly convinced in your heart of hearts that you can trust those words? Do you trust God's word for you? Check out Psalm 32 and see if it works for you.

> Blessed is the person whose short-fall is forgiven
> Blessed is the person whose sin is cleansed
> Blessed is the person to whom God imputes no iniquity.
> Blessed is the person in whose spirit there is no guile.
> Be happy in God's grace and rejoice
> All you whom God has declared righteous.
> Shout for joy all you whom God has declared saintly in heart.

For God's Pleasure and Purpose

It is clear that the only thing that keeps us trapped in our neurotic fear, guilt, and shame is our own negative psychology. God has tried hard to deliver us from it. What else can God do than announce unconditional divine grace and universal forgiveness forever for everything for everybody? Some folks think this announcement is mythic mysticism, believing that what counts is the happiness one derives from acquiring material comfort and the money and power to control all the possible inadvertencies in life. They think that he who has the most toys when he dies wins.

Sometimes we get this impression from Hollywood celebrities whose lives are full of material riches and who seem to go around with empty heads, false goals, fruitless relationships, and achievements that do not really count for anything. Pitiable in the extreme! Does that seem inviting to you? Is that what you idealize as your source of meaning? We were not made mainly for fame but for inner growth, so we can blossom psycho-spiritually every future minute and for all eternity.

It is my experience that authentic people, grounded in substantive values, want honesty, honor, loyalty, hope, and idealism. God wants that too—for us and for our world. Too many political candidates seem to want power, fame, money, and immunity from responsibility. Perhaps you have read *The Kite Runner* by Khaled Hosseini. I cannot figure out why so many people thought that book was so extraordinary, however, it makes a central point very well. The main character, who had the option of greed, narcissism, manipulation of a friend, and trivialization of his family, learned through pain the value of loyalty, hope, and idealism. He put his life on the line to rescue a brother in need from the tragic treachery of the Taliban.

My father was a farmer and an engineer. He taught me how to plow a straight furrow with a walking plow. He told me that the only way to plow correctly in a broad field is to "identify an object such as a tree on the far end of the field. Start the horses in that direction and keep your eye on that objective. Look only forward and never look back." It reminded me of Jesus' observation, "He who puts his hand to the plow and looks back is unworthy of me" (Luke 9:62). I discovered that if you look back you cannot help but move the plow handles to the right or left and that makes the moldboard of the plow swerve out of the furrow and makes it crooked. Keep your eye on the objective and what is behind you will take care of itself. The furrow will be straight.

Taking the short view and looking back makes a crooked furrow in life. God owns what is behind us and guarantees that our path will be straightened by God's forgiving grace. If we keep our focus on the past we will not keep our eye on the objective. We will not concentrate on the present process and we will have no future before us. God takes pleasure in God's people. God enjoys straightening out our past and inviting us into the objectives before us. This unfolding of history is, after all, God's ingenious experiment. It is a win-win world. No one will fall out of God's grace. When the time comes for us and we fall off the edge, we fall into the arms of divine grace. We are made for God's pleasure and the entire enterprise of God's provident and redeeming grace is a great delight to God.

God invites us always to take God's long-term vision of things. We are urged to celebrate our forgiveness and God's busy dry-cleaning of our history. God looks at us every day and cannot remember that we are failed and flawed creatures. God thinks we are saints because our lives are constantly dry-cleaned by God's automatic forgiveness. We were made for God's good pleasure, the Psalmist says in our text. That thought is intended to move us to glorify God according to the psalm.

I suppose that idea means that while we make our way before the face of God and under pressure of eternity, we are invited to worship God, praise God, thank God, and keep that eternal focus. George Bernard Shaw was an interesting English poet of the last century. He said that the true joy of life is to be used up for a purpose recognized by ourselves as a mighty one. He thought the meaning in life was in being a force of nature instead of a feverish and selfish little clot of ailments and grievances, complaining that the world will not devote itself to making us happy.

In my psychotherapy clinic I often see people who live only for themselves and for the moment. They come for counseling because they are miserable. They have no ideal focus and no satisfaction or meaning in life. Narcissism is its own miserable reward. What do you see as the focused force driving your life? Would those who know you say the same? Would it look like that to your family? Each of us probably ought to test that and see what it looks like to those near and around us. That might cause you to adjust your sails closer to the wind of the Divine Spirit. What would you do differently with your life if it really dawned on you that you are going to last forever—longer after death than before it? How would you adjust your sails in the winds of life if you really downloaded into your heart of hearts the realization that God takes great pleasure in guaranteeing you a blessed and saintly time and eternity?

Amen. So let it Be!

SERMON SEVENTEEN

Be Transformed
—Romans 12:1-13

Do not conform, transform!

— ROMANS 12:2

ROMANS 12:2 ENJOINS US not to be conformed to this world but to be transformed by the renewing of our minds. I recently saw the French film, *Chocolat*. If you have not seen it you should. If we could show it here this morning I would not need to preach this sermon. That film is the closest thing to the proclamation of the essential gospel from Romans 12 that we have on film. The funny side of it is that the main character in the end is spiritually saved and redeemed, *transformed by chocolate*. Go and see it.

Constantine took over the Christian church in 313 CE. In 325 CE he transformed the church into a theological and political institution by convening the first really ecumenical council. He gathered all the bishops and instructed them to develop a doctrinal creed and orthodox theology for the Christian church. Then he gave into the hands of the bishops the control of both the church and the empire. He introduced a practice that in many parts of the church persists to this day during the season of Lent.

That is the practice of celebrating a season of forty days of fasting, prayer, and sacrifice leading to Holy Week. It is commemorative of Jesus' suffering, thus a season of repentance.

That was one of the first disciplines imposed upon the Imperial Church. It linked Jesus' suffering to our suffering. It was intended as a liturgy for us to show sorrow for our sinfulness. It implied an emphasis upon our personal sacrifice to atone for our sins! That notion of adding our sacrifice to the sacrifice of Christ, as a resolution of the problem of our sinfulness, became entrenched in the church.

There is, of course, a rationale for this development in the church. There are scriptural imperatives about the Christian life. John the Baptist preached on the shores of the Jordan River upon the central theme of repentance: *Repent for the reign of God is exploding upon you right now.* (Matt 3:2). Practically the first thing Jesus says in Luke's gospel is "Repent and believe" (Luke 13:4). When Jesus told the story of the eighteen people that were killed inadvertently when the tower of Siloam toppled over, he said, *Let this be a lesson to you. They were no more or less sinful than anybody else on the face of the earth and therefore the tower might as well have fallen on you as on them, so repent or perish* (Luke 13:4).

In Luke 24 Jesus said that repentance and remission of sins should be preached in his name to all the nations. In 1 Corinthians 11:23–29, the passage we recite at the communion table, Paul remarks about commemorating the suffering of Jesus. The bottom line there is "do this in remembrance of me." Paul intimates that these are words from the mouth of the Jesus himself.

Scripture gives some kind of rationale to this early development regarding Lent in the thought of the church. For example, scripture lays upon us the commands of Christian behavior change. James says, "Faith without works is dead. You show me your faith apart from your works and I will show you my faith by my works." Surely there is something of that behind Paul's remark in our text today, "Be not conformed to this world but be transformed by renewing your mind." Jesus was constantly teaching us a new way of thought and behavior. He set those forth by his words and actions. In the epistle to the Hebrews all of that is expressed in a few words declaring that Jesus was worthy to be our savior because he was made perfect through suffering. So you can see that the early church perceived that the pressure was on to transform the past Roman world from its pagan spiritual roots to that of transformed and transforming Christians. It is not surprising that the emphasis fell upon repentance and obedience. That was viewed as personal payment for misbehavior in the early Catholic Church. That tradition persisted throughout the Middle Ages and into our day. It did not really change until the Second Vatican Council was convened by Pope John XXIII. Since the ascendancy of Benedict XVI the practice has been rolled back to pre-Vatican II orthodox traditions in the Roman Catholic Church. Unfortunately, the ancient church's erroneous modes and meanings have been restored by Benedict XVI.

Luther discovered the passage in Ephesians that says, "By grace you are saved, through faith, and that not of yourselves it is a gift of God, not of works lest anyone should boast that he can do it on his own" (Eph 2:8–9). With that the church was off to a very new and authentic Christian beginning. Luther, John Calvin, John Knox, Philipp Melancthon, and Ulrich Zwingli were the great reformers of the church in the sixteenth century. They saw one thing clearly. They saw that Christianity is a way of life that is by grace alone. They perceived that what Lent stood for and what the whole call to Christian life stood for was not at all penitence and payment for sin, but rather a new way of looking at spirituality. Not payment and penitence but review and revision of our faith and our life.

Today all Christendom, except some hard core Fundamentalist Evangelicals, see that a theology prescribing that we work our way into God's favor is pagan. It cuts the very tap root of God's grace as expressed in the gospel. The Second Vatican Council brought fresh air blowing through the Roman Catholic Church. Unfortunately, under the regimes of Pope John Paul II and Pope Benedict XVI the Catholic Church has regressed radically to a kind of medieval perspective in theology and liturgy. That is a great loss for the world.

You and I are invited by the good news of the gospel to see that celebrating our freedom in God's radical grace and total forgiveness leads healthy Christians to say spontaneously, *If that is the way God feels about me then I want to be God's kind of person. I want to behave like one of God's people.* We still live in the context of these two strains of historic faith. One of them is legalistic and emphasizes penitence and payment for sin. The other celebrates God's free grace and emphasizes review and revision of our lives under the light of the word of God. In the latter context obedience and transformed behavior have concrete and substantial meaning for true believers.

By Grace Alone

Romans 12 does not enjoin us to behavior designed to show God how nice we are. Christian life is not about how we can manipulate God to favor and forgive us because of our painful sacrifice. Christian life is behavior transformed by the gratitude of a soul re-directed by God's forgiveness. It is the expression of a spirit transformed by the love of godliness. The Christian way is a life changed by the urge to be in God's business in the precarious context of the tragic destiny of this complicated world.

In the days of King Arthur, six centuries after Christ, the Roman Empire was rapidly collapsing. The story of King Arthur was the story of a dignified and civilized Roman from Britain, hanging on by his teeth and toenails, so to speak, to the great virtues and values of the Roman Empire, while all of Continental Europe, North Africa, and Rome itself had been overrun by the Barbarian Germanic hordes. It was the end of civilization in Europe, as it had been known in the Greco-Roman times.

King Arthur was desperately endeavoring to preserve a little island of civilization in Britain and on the northern coast of France. In those desperate days, two English brothers fell into bad company and afoul of the law for thievery. They had stolen a farmer's sheep. In that progressively barbaric time they were caught and branded on their foreheads as sheep thieves. A brand that burned into the flesh of their foreheads the letters ST: sheep thief. One in shame ran away, lived a profligate life, alienated himself from society, burned in his soul by the brand on his head, and died in destitution. He was buried in a pauper's grave somewhere in northern France, it is said.

Initially the other was tempted to do the same, but instead he determined to correct his life. He had been touched as a child by the story of Peter's forgiveness at the Sea of Galilee, after denying Jesus three times. The thief saw it as his only chance. He changed his mind. He worked to pay for the stolen sheep and to make restitution sevenfold as the scripture commands. He spent his life in caring for the needy in his village, in teaching the young, and in assisting the local priest with training the children in the faith. He transformed himself by the renewing of his mind. He distributed the proceeds of his farm for the care of the indigent and for the support of the abbey just across the border in Cornwall.

Time passed. His contemporaries passed on. He lived to a surprising old age and he became in fact a legend in his own time. No one really noticed anymore the brand on his forehead: ST. It just seemed like a natural birthmark to everyone in the village. People never thought about it for generations. He became the model that people thought of as a Christian.

One day a naive child, who had not noticed the brand before, was suddenly able to make out the two letters, ST. He was astounded by it and asked his middle-aged father what that meant: ST. His father was equally surprised to notice it again and he said, "I don't really know. I can't remember anybody ever saying, but from the time I was a little child I guess we always thought that it meant *Saint*." Be not conformed to this world. Be transformed by the changing of your minds. The lessons of Lent are not penitence and payment but review and revision. Be transformed.

    Amen. So let it Be!

SERMON EIGHTEEN

Christians as Theologians
—Ezra 7:6–10; Matthew 22:15–17a

> Ezra set his heart to study the word of God.
> — Ezra 7:10

> We know you teach the word of God truthfully.
> — Matthew 22:16b

EVERY BELIEVER OR SPIRITUAL inquirer is a theologian. Whether we intend it, are conscious of it, or realize it, we are all theologians. That is, we are all inevitably engaged in the pursuit of knowing more and more about God. Moreover, we all have a strong motivation to get it right: to understand God accurately.

Ezra was a theologian. The Bible says he was skilled in the word of the Lord. He had a heart to study the word from the God. Moreover, he went at this enterprise of the truth quest with intentionality and vigor. This was not merely a casual undertaking for him, an occasional Sunday afternoon read.

It was the conscious and willful hard work of focused study. Ezra's desire to know about God stood in contrast to that of the Scribes and Pharisees who questioned Jesus. They were also theologians. They were asking questions about God and God's will for us. They acted like they wanted to know about God and to know God. Knowing about God and knowing God are, of course, two quite different matters. However, the New Testament describes the true motivation of those religious leaders. It claims that they were not interested in a quest for divine and eternal truth. They were interested only in an intellectual debate. Whether that is true, it is the perspective of the gospel authors. The religious leaders of the Jews had come to catch Jesus in a theological trap.

It is not uncommon for religious devotees to engage in mere intellectual debate about God rather than join together in an honest theological quest for truth. Throughout the history of Christianity the church has had many lay theologians. Indeed, every member is one in some sense. We have also had many important professional theologians. During the last two hundred years two of the most important professional theologians were Friedrich Schleiermacher, who lived at the beginning of the nineteenth century, and Karl Barth, who lived during the twentieth century.

Barth criticized Schleiermacher severely. Of course, Schleiermacher was already dead by that time. Barth believed that God revealed God's self to us only in the Bible and he disagreed with Schleiermacher's idea that God was revealing God's self to us all the time. Schleiermacher thought God is revealed in the intricacies of creation and in the guidance and blessings of providence. Moreover, he was sure that God is revealed in the personal human experiences of the intimations and illuminations from the Divine Spirit. These come to us all through life, he thought, in those moments when we just know that some surprising understanding or event is a moment *of the Spirit*.

Barth wrote a long list of huge volumes about God. He was very busy with the theological quest of knowing *about* God. Schleiermacher was trying to get beyond merely knowing about God and getting to *know* God. His theology was an attempt to describe what it is like to know God after you know enough about God to discern God's Spirit's presence in the special moments of intimation and illumination in everyday life. Barth was very good at describing God with ideas that stood outside of the heart and spirit of the believer, entering at best only into the mind. Schleiermacher thought that theology should help the Christian to experience God's presence in the inner person, internalized as personal spirituality—a thing of the heart.

All of us have had moments when we heard some idea or theory and responded by thinking that it sounded pretty good, but found ourselves not quite accepting it as yet for truth. We held it out there at arm's length, so to speak. We were not thoroughly convinced. That is quite different from the spontaneous experience of finding an insight or illumination entering into us with a strong sense of conviction that this really is a correct notion—indeed, the truth. We cannot push and shove our way to get to those illuminations. They come to us from the Divine Spirit. Schleiermacher wanted to cultivate that inner experience of God. He was sure that the Spirit of God was alive and well and working everywhere to insinuate into our consciousness the illuminations of God's truth and God's way for all of us. He was sure that in a posture of prayer and meditation, sailing close to the wind of the Spirit, so to speak, we open ourselves to such convincing truth from God.

He did not mean that the Spirit of God speaks in *any* wild notion that comes into our heads or hearts. The intimations of the Spirit are not random shots in this *wild* world, but they are tutored insights that ring true to what we know of God in creation, providence, the Bible, the historic faith of the church, and the healing power of forgiving grace.

That is, theology is not just a recitation of propositions about God's nature, behavior, or will for us. Ezra did not limit himself to reciting propositions about God. The Bible says he set his heart to study the word of God, to do the word of God, and to teach the word of God. That is, he decided consciously to make God's truth his own, a thing of the heart, a reality of truth inside himself. Out of that he spoke and believed and lived. Many of you have taken or are taking Bible study courses. In that you are doing exactly what Ezra undertook to do.

Incorporating God's truth as it is made convincing to our hearts by the Spirit of God is not just a matter of theological theory or propositions, of logic and argument. It is about living and celebrating life in the Spirit. It is more than knowing about God. It is the personal experience of knowing God. Sometimes in churches—indeed, in our church—we have a debate between whether being a Christian is about knowing theology or doing the work of caring for the world. That is a false construction of the theological quest for God's truth and God's authentic way for us.

As for Ezra, being God's person is to intentionally make the conscious decision to *know*, and to *believe*. Internalizing the experiences of the Spirit empowers us *to do* the things of God. For Ezra it all ended with the ministry of teaching. We might call it witnessing or evangelism. Christians sometimes seem afraid of witnessing to the presence and work of God in the world. It is actually an easy thing to share the intimations of the Spirit. It merely requires that we watch for opportunities in our own or other's lives in which God seems to be moving in a special way. Then it seems completely appropriate and gratifying to say boldly, "That looks like it is of the Spirit!" Let us be aware of those moments and call attention to those revelations of the Spirit all the time. Then we will see the Spirit moving when we least expect it. It will become a way of life to watch for how God will show up as the Divine Spirit around the next corner.

Moreover, it is always good to remember that people do not *care* how much you *know* until they *know* how much you *care*. I am always conscious of the fact that I am called to be a professional theologian, as well as a Christian seeking to know God personally. I am a good theologian. I know a lot about God and about a lot of other things. However, I always find it refreshing to remind myself that people do not care how much I know until they know how much I care about them. Knowing, believing, and doing are one thing!

Amen. So let it Be!

SERMON NINETEEN

God's Mountain
—Psalm 48:1–2, Samuel 5:1–5, 5:9–10

> God is greatly to be praised on God's Holy Mountain . . . tell the next generation.
> — Psalm 48:1, 48:13

WE HAVE A BELOVED hymn entitled, "Christ is Made a Sure Foundation." We often sing it as a prayer for illumination. It is a celebration of the church. In it the church is referred to as Holy Zion and described as built on the foundation of Christ as its cornerstone. The church's hymnody, from ancient times to the present, has always been rich with such metaphors. For example, you can find many such hymns full of biblical metaphors for the church, going all the way back to the beginning. We have a hymn which declares that God is going to build up the walls of Zion. That means that God will cause the church on earth to flourish. Many colorful metaphors are used in the Bible and in our hymns to describe the attributes of Christ's church, the community of believers. For example, such figures as City of God, City of the Lord of Hosts, Holy Mountain, Mt. Zion, City of David, New Jerusalem, Holy City, and the New Israel are used in the Bible and in our hymns to describe the church.

God's Mountain

In Galatians 6:16 we read of the fellowship of the faithful, "Peace and mercy be . . . upon the Israel of God." Psalm 125:1 declares of the community of believers, "Those who trust in the Lord are like Mt. Zion, which cannot be moved but is established forever." I have a friend at the University of Michigan, Professor Yaron Eliav, who published a book entitled, *God's Mountain*. It is a nice book about Mt. Zion, that is, the Temple Mount in Jerusalem. That is the top of that mountain on which the ancient Israelite temples stood in Jerusalem, known then as the Holy City. Today the Mosque of Omar and the magnificent Dome of the Rock stand there.

To Abraham that spot was known as Mt. Moriah. To David it was Mt. Zion and the City of David. From Solomon to Jesus people called it the Temple of God or just the Temple. For Paul it had come to be the Holy City. For the author of the Book of Revelation (which is attributed to John), it was known as the symbol of the New Jerusalem. So in Revelation 3:12, 21:2–3 and 21:10, we read of the church, "I will make you a pillar in the temple of my God; . . . I will write on you the name of my God, and the name of the city of my God, the New Jerusalem which comes down from God out of heaven . . . . Behold, the dwelling place of God is with humankind . . . . We shall be his people and God himself shall be with us."

In these metaphoric celebrations of the church, what do we mean to be saying? What did Jesus, Paul, and John intend? In the Old Testament Jerusalem became known as God's special city. That is a very ancient notion. In the earliest records of the Hebrew people there is a figure named Melchizedek whom Abraham encountered. He was known already before the time of Abraham as the King of Salem and a priest of the Most High God. His city was called Salem, the City of Peace and the Mountain of God. It was later called Jerusalem by King David because he took it from the Jebusites in 1000 BCE and so named it Jebu-salem, modified to Jerusalem because it is easier to pronounce.

For David, it was always thought of as Salem, City of Peace, and the place where God lived. So after David had consolidated the kingdom of Israel and built himself a palace of cedar wood, he looked into building a temple and bringing the Ark of the Covenant up from the tent of Obed-Edom to Jerusalem. He wanted to install it in the Temple on Mt. Zion. Solomon actually eventually built that temple but David brought the Ark of the Covenant up to Mt Zion as the symbol of the special Divine Presence there. He established it in a temporary tabernacle until the temple was completed. Mt. Zion was thought to be the place where God lived.

By Grace Alone

Still today Jews, Christians, and Muslims view that spot on Mt. Zion as a sacred and holy place. Thus for Christians, metaphorically, the Church as God's special place of presence on earth, God's sanctuary, is celebrated in scriptures and hymns as holy, sacred, aflame with the Holy Spirit symbolized by our candles, characterized by special decorum, and referred to as Mt. Zion. It symbolizes a special space where the worshipping community formally meets God.

Where do we get this notion of God especially present in such a special place or amongst a special people? Everybody knows that God is omnipresent. God is equally present everywhere. Why a special congregation, a special building, or sanctuary? Why a special space, shape, liturgy, or decorum? We do not need to come to church to be with God. Jesus himself declared that when we pray we should go into a closet where we can be alone with God. Jesus apparently seldom went to temple or synagogue and he knew nothing, of course, of a church.

One does not need to be a church member or attend church in order to be a Christian. At present it seems nearly impossible to inspire youth—sons and daughters of the church and children of devoted parents—to perceive the importance of time in sacred space. There seems to be decreasing consciousness of the importance of time with God and God's people in the sanctuary. We need to ask this question again with more urgency, Why a church? Why be part of a congregation?

Well, the answer is not all that obscure. I remember my father telling me of an old man in his church who had been a great leader and elder in his day, but he grew old. He found himself a bit out of the mainstream. That upset him. New things were being done in the church. He did not like the changes so he stopped coming to church. After a couple of weeks of this most uncharacteristic behavior on the part of this old saint of God, the pastor went to see him. The old man sat in silence before his fire. The pastor arrived but the old man did not speak. They sat together in silence for an hour watching the fire.

In the middle of that very nice fire was a large coal burning hot and bright. It practically kept the entire fire going. The occasional blasts of winter wind down the chimney could not quench it. After a while the pastor got up and with the poker teased the big red hot coal out of the fire. He pushed it into the far corner of the fireplace. Then he sat down again in silence for another hour. The fire continued to burn but that big red hot coal, off by itself, cooled and died. The pastor rose silently and left. Next Sunday the old man was back in church.

God's Mountain

It is true that you do not need to come to church to be a Christian, but what if you do not? A boy and his father were walking along the seashore on vacation. They were celebrating the beauty of the sand, the sky, the sun, and the sea. Suddenly the boy looked at his new watch and said, "Dad, it is Sunday morning and it is nearly 10:00. We should be in church." His father said, "That would be nice but look at the beauty of God's great creation here in the sun, the sand, and the sea, under God's magnificent blue sky. We can praise and worship God just as well here in nature as we can in church." The boy said, "Yes, I know, Dad, we can—but we won't will we?"

We go to church for worship because we experience some special sense of God's presence in church: in the building and in the congregation of people. Moreover, that sense of things moves us to certain behaviors. It prompts special functions and a special sense of the Divine Spirit. It has something to do with experiencing God's Spirit present to our own spirits. That experience is fairly hard to get elsewhere. Here we are immune to the distractions of life for a little while. We have dedicated this sacred space of sanctuary to the experience of mutuality with each other and with God.

The scientists who worked on the Manhattan Project in World War II were surprised by a new insight they discovered. As they developed the nuclear bombs they found out that you must create what is called a critical mass if the bomb is to ignite. A nuclear bomb requires critical mass. That is, to make a hydrogen bomb you need to assemble just the right amount and concentration of the right kind of nuclear fuel. Then you must set off an atomic bomb to incite the explosion of that critical mass igniting the hydrogen bomb.

The special sense of God being present in the church building and with the church as congregation is like a critical mass of presence here. It takes that critical mass to set our own spirits going with the tunes, tremors, and intimations of God as Spirit. That is why we sing the hymn:

> O holy city, seen of John, where Christ, the Lamb, does reign
> Within whose foursquare walls shall come, no night, nor need, nor pain
> And where the tears are wiped from eyes that shall not weep again!
> Give us, O God, the strength to build, The City that has stood,
> Too long a dream, whose laws are love, whose ways are servant-hood.
> And where the sun that shines becomes God's grace for human good.
> Already in the mind of God that city rises fair,
> Lo, how its splendor challenges the souls that greatly dare,
> And bids us seize the whole of life and build its glory there.

By Grace Alone

Critical Mass: God especially present in and to the worshipping community. Nice words! What do they mean? First, I think they mean that it is here that we pursue the truth with intentionality. God's truth! The truth of the meaning of our lives! This is the place of our quest, our discernment, our acquiring the truth. Here is the root and ground of our practice of the truth. Second, I think that here we find the focus and tone of our true selves; our care, our concern, and our mutuality in Spirit. Here we learn and express our cherishing of each other, cherishing of our world, and cherishing of the things of God. Third, here we learn the language of celebration: the warm-hearted appreciation of God's creation, providence, goodwill, grace, mercy, and forgiveness. These are the central things of our fundamental need for time and eternity.

Fourth, it is here, therefore, that we find our true and authentic identity. We are the ones who get up, stand up, and march up to Mt. Zion, to the City of our God. It is our sanctuary. We come with purpose and intention to the Holy Place, the sanctuary. This is our sacred space. Here is the font where we are marked with God's mark, and the table of our nurturance with God's bread and wine. We are the ones who stand for, stand up for, and rejoice to hear the Word proclaimed. We are the ones identified as those who stand for the Bible. It is the source of spiritual refreshment, as significant for us as life and breath. Coming to this sanctuary for worship is like coming up for air when swimming in the rough waters of life.

Fifth, here we find our focused mutual motivation, expressed so beautifully in our hymn entitled, appropriately, "Come Labor On." Finally, here we find the quiet place where we can savor the flavor of that life of quiet humility we all long for, with its security and tranquility. This is the one place in the world where defensiveness is unnecessary.

Of course, the church is not *necessary*, but it is a wonderful opportunity, an unspeakable gift. It is a congenial setting for sensing the critical mass of the divine, present in our spirits. Here we feel ourselves being tuned again with God's Spirit after a week in the ruckus of the world. Where else can you get that? That is the opportunity so many are missing, and we must boldly let them know that fact, lest they fail themselves, humanity, and God.

Amen! So let it Be!

SERMON TWENTY

God Rested

—Genesis 1–2:3; Exodus 20:8–11; Hebrews 4:4, 4:9–11a

> On the seventh day God finished the work and rested.
> — Genesis 2:2–3

> There is a rest for the people of God.
> — Hebrews 4:9

> On the seventh day you shall not do any work.
> —Exodus 20:8–11

RECENTLY A MAN CONTACTED me who describes himself as a Christian, who is also a scientist. He is a dogmatic creationist who wrote me a long email on why I should be a creationist and not an evolutionist. He must have read one of my books to know I am an evolutionist. There is a lot of sound and fury these days about the subject of creation and evolution. Most of it is worthless, signifying nothing.

You know the creation story in Genesis 1 so well that no one needs to reread it for you. If I share with you just a few sentences, the entire story will return to your mind. It says, of course, that in the beginning God created the heavens and the earth. It took him six long eras. Then God looked over all that God had made and noted that it was a really good job. At that point God reflected upon creating humans, and decided to create us in God's likeness. So God created us like God in a number of key ways. We are sexual beings capable of creating and recreating life. Then God decided to put us in charge, tying God's own hands, so to speak, by declaring, *You be fruitful and multiply and replenish the earth. Have dominion over it. Creatively make it achieve all the fruitful potential with which I have invested it as creator* (Gen 1:28). God put us in charge and does not muck around in our business.

You know that entire story, written in such beautiful ancient Hebrew poetry. You may not know that there are two creation stories in the Bible. Genesis 1 has one story and Genesis 2 has a quite different one. Since this situation was sort of awkward to the ancient editor of the book of Genesis, he or she formulated a neat transitional paragraph between the two stories. That transitional paragraph is Genesis 2:1–3. Our text comes from the last of those verses, "God rested."

Now, of course, those two words are a metaphor, a word-picture, a figure of speech. That metaphor is built upon an anthropomorphism, that is, upon words describing human types of experiences and functions. These anthropomorphisms are projected upon the notion of God in the creation stories. The dogmatic creationist who wrote me the email, however, takes sentences like that in the Bible completely literally. He wants me to understand that it is not so much that the Bible describes God as designed after our image, but rather that we must remember that we behave after the way God behaves. God literally rested after six days of hard work and we should rest after six days of hard work each week. He takes a second text, from Exodus 20:8–11, to prove that his literal reading is accurate and my metaphorical one is wrong.

For this reason he insists that this material world came into existence by six twenty-four hour days of direct and immediate creative activity by

God and that was that. He is certain that all the scientific evidence from geology and archaeology for the progressive development of organisms from less complex to more complex ones over long eras of time is simply not the truth and should not be taken seriously. He thinks that evolution only *seems* like an accurate description of the scientific data because of the false assumption about evolution instead of creation with which ungodly scientists come at the data and formulate theories about it.

His most important point, however, is that if you speak of God using evolution as the divine method of creation, you cave in to secular and ungodly theories about the world. These theories inevitably erode your sense of the majestic presence of God in your life. It whittles away at your true spirituality, he says, and makes you unable to take literally the message of Jesus Christ as the exclusive way to salvation. He is sure that my position as a theistic evolutionist, that is, one who believes that God created this world by a carefully designed process of evolution, will water down and erode my authentic spirituality.

That Christian scientist needs a God who literally works six days and rests one, or he is sure he will not have a God who saves him in the three literal days of Jesus' crucifixion, death and resurrection. After all, says he, the Ten Commandments tell us that we must remember the Sabbath day to keep it sacred: six days we shall do all our work and the seventh day no one may work, because in six days God created all things and rested the seventh day, blessing the Sabbath day and making it sacred.

Unfortunately, the fellow seems to have missed the fact that the first form of the Ten Commandments to be written is in Deuteronomy 5, where keeping the Sabbath has nothing whatsoever to do with God working six days and resting the seventh. There the reason to keep the Sabbath is that the relief from work symbolizes the Exodus and the deliverance from the slave labor that the Israelites endured in Egypt.

Nonetheless, this metaphor about God's rest, when seen as a word-picture of God's life in eternity, takes on an altogether different kind of import as we move into the New Testament. The author of Hebrews would have disagreed vigorously with the literal interpretation of the dogmatic creationist. In Hebrews 4:4 and 9–11a, the author picks up from Genesis 2:3 the idea that God rested, and recognizing it as a metaphor uses it to encourage us in the spiritual pilgrimage of our earthly journey. He or she uses it to encourage us to continually reach out to achieve the rest God has prepared for us, i.e., a rest which will become complete when we go to be with the Lord eternally. The author of that epistle links this metaphor with the Exodus again, as did the original form of the Ten Commandments in Deuteronomy 5. He or she says that our entering into our eternal rest is symbolized by the Israelite people of God entering into the promised land of Canaan, to have a prosperous life in the "land of milk and honey" (Exod 3:8, 3;17). That was to be a life filled with God's Shalom (total prosperity in body, mind, and spirit)!

Building upon that extension of the word picture, Hebrews declares with assurance, *There is now, therefore, a rest for the people of God . . . . Let us ensure that we enter into that rest which God has prepared for us. Let us not fall short of it like those rebellious Israelites who died in the wilderness and did not enter into the Promised Land* (Heb 4:9, 4:11)

Now if you have really been listening to me for the years of my ministry with you, you are going to be tempted to say at this point, "Dr. Ellens, you have just caught yourself in your own trap. You preach that grace is unconditional, radical, and universal and that we cannot sin ourselves out of God's grace. You claim that we cannot squirm out of God's long embrace. So what about this business of failing to enter into God's eternal rest?" You pose the right question. It is a simple and direct one. The answer is as simple and as direct. You need to recall all that I have said to you about Paul's doctrine of eternal life. It is a quality concept and not a quantity concept. *Everlasting life* refers to life that goes on forever. Paul developed the wonderful insight of *eternal life* as quite a different experience: life on God's plane that begins right now and continues throughout our lives here and after death. Not everyone lives life on God's plane here and now, but Paul repeatedly makes it clear that everyone will when in the transition from life to eternity we all see and confess Christ as Lord.

God rested, metaphorically. That poetic line creates a word picture of what we can expect of life with God and with his Spirit in the world. We can achieve the rest God has for us. We are invited to enter into it right here and now, to enter into that life on God's plane, immediately, 1) by utter trust in God's unconditional goodwill for us; 2) by utter trust in God's forgiveness for us all before we were born and for everything forevermore; 3) by utter trust in the Divine Spirit to guide and illumine us in palpable and tangible experiences day by day in all our life now and forever and 4)by utter trust that death will be a mere step across a small threshold into the fullness of that rest for all eternity.

The poor guy who wrote me the email needs his literal dogmatic creationism and salvation theories because he has not yet come to see and trust God's grace. Moreover, he is hung up on dogmatic misinterpretations of specially selected proof texts from scripture, because it has not dawned upon him that this is the age of the Spirit that wants to lead him into all God's truth. He has not learned to trust the Divine Spirit to give him security, truth, certainty, illumination day by day, and biblical peace. He has not yet entered into the grace of God's rest: the assurance of God's unconditional grace and forgiveness of everybody, for everything, for evermore. Have you?

There remains a rest for the people of God. Let us enter into that rest now, achieving Paul's kind of eternal life on God's plane of reality during this life. Then eternity will be a continuation of the same confident security. This is the prize you do not need to be dead to win. It nullifies the deadliness of death. It is the restful peace of real living, which we may enjoy while we are alive, here and now!

Amen. So let it Be!

SERMON TWENTY ONE

A Snake in the Desert

—Numbers 21:4–9; John 3:14–21, 8:28; 12:32–34;
Ephesians 2:4–10

When I am lifted up on the cross you will know that I am the One.
— John 8:28

To show the immeasurable riches of God's grace
through cherishing us in Christ Jesus.
— Ephesians 2:7

The story of the snake in the desert in Numbers 21 is a strange story. Therefore, Jesus' remarks about it make for a strange story, as well. At God's command Moses put a metal snake on a stick to deliver the Israelites from their sickness and the fear they all had about their sickness. Jesus claimed that, just so, the Son of Man must be lifted up upon a stake in the ground to deliver all humanity from our sickness: fear, guilt, and shame. John says

A Snake in the Desert

that Jesus was referring to his crucifixion. This was necessary for Jesus in order to get the job done that he needed to get done, a job which was a little like the job Moses had to get done.

Moses put that bronze snake on a pole so that everyone could look at it. The Israelites had wandered into a part of the wilderness infested by snakes and many Israelites were bitten by the snakes. Either from the poison of the snakes or from the fear that the snakes were poisonous, some Israelites died. We cannot tell from the story how serious the snake bites really were, but it is clear that it scared the daylights out of the entire congregation of Israelites, and for some it scared the life out of them. They were terrified of the snakes and God said that the solution was a snake. The problem is the snakes. The solution is the snake.

Now how did that bronze snake that Moses lifted up on a pole cure those Israelites? I suppose we ought to take this story with a sense of humor. It is a story which may or may not have happened in history. By the time it got written into the Bible it was an old, old legend. The important thing about it is not that it is an old legend but that it describes what faith is like. The Israelites had a problem. They were poisoned in body or spirit by snakes. God said, *Look at the snake and you will be cured!*

What was it about the bronze snake that cured them? Was it some kind of magic? Absolutely not! It was not a magic snake. It was just a dumb piece of cold metal on a stick. Was it some sort of special energy that came out of that bronze snake like some New Age folks say these days? They keep magical rocks, pyramids, crystals, and all sorts of weird things in their homes that are supposed to emit health enhancing energy, and make them wiser, happier, more wholesome persons. I have never seen anyone that seemed to profit from such things, though I have noticed that a lot of such folks really ought to be given *something* to improve their attitudes and natures.

All those New Age magical things are bunk, of course. Was this snake also just bunk? Well, it was not just bunk, we know, because God said, *Turn your face to my snake. If you turn your face to my snake you are going to be fine.* So they turned their faces toward the snake and they were fine. Sounds like some weird pagan ritual, does it not? What are we to make of it? It was not some special quality of that snake. It was not magic. It was not some energy coming out of the metal and into them to cure them.

It was the simple fact that they trusted God's promise. It had to do with which way they turned their faces. That is what faith is! They trusted God's promise because they had the faith in which they trusted that what

God said could be counted on. They heard God say, *I want to heal you. The way I am going to do it is by this symbolic snake. Look at the snake and believe that it symbolizes that I am going to heal you. That is what the symbolic snake on the pole stands for! Look at it, trust me, open your mind and heart to my healing.*

That is what faith is about. They turned their face to God's symbol and were healed, relieved of their fear and sickness. What healed them was, of course, the fact that they trusted God's word. They trusted God's promise. They recognized the promise represented in God's symbol. So their trust implied that they believed that God wanted to heal them, that God is a healer, and that the snake was God's symbol for their healing. It was their faith in God's intent regarding them that healed them.

That is why Jesus said that "As Moses lifted up the serpent in the wilderness, so also must the Son of Man be lifted up" (John 3:14). This is a really awesome thing for Jesus to say. It is awesome because it turns upside down all the atonement theology of the last twenty centuries of Christian history. Think about it for a minute. Jesus is saying that there is no special energy flowing from his crucifixion to save us. This even puts in jeopardy Paul's remark that Jesus' crucifixion was a propitiation for our sins. It certainly overturns the notion of Anselm that somehow or other this business of crucifixion is so virtuous a thing for Jesus to go through that it stacks up a reservoir of virtue that we can draw upon to balance the scales of our sin and lack of virtue.

Jesus says that when we see the Son of Man lifted up, then we will know that he is the one. The one what? He is the one who is the symbol that God has set up for us to see. He is the symbol of our healing toward which we are invited to turn our faces in faith. That faith is simply the trust that God is in *Christ* reconciling us and the whole world unto God's self. Jesus says the crucifixion is a symbol of God's passion for us. As the snake in the desert was a symbol of God's passion for healing the Israelites, so the crucified Christ is God's symbol for God's passion for our spiritual healing—our utter uncalculated forgiveness and acceptance for time and eternity.

The gospel tells us another interesting story that illustrates this in a wonderful, maybe even humorous way. You remember the time that Peter walked on the water. From his boat Peter saw Jesus on the shore of the Sea of Galilee. As soon as he recognized that it was Jesus he jumped out of the boat and began to walk on the water to embrace Jesus. When he got halfway to shore he suddenly realized what he was actually doing in his ecstatic enthusiasm. He was walking on water! He began to wonder about himself. He looked down at the water and the waves and as soon as he became preoccupied with himself and his danger he began to sink.

The Bible says that then he turned his face toward the Lord and cried out, "Lord, help me. I perish." Of course, he was then immediately and safely ashore. That is a definition of saving faith. He turned his face to the Lord. He did not kneel down and confess his sins. He did not recite the Apostles' Creed. He would not have had time to do so, even if he had known the Apostles' Creed, which, of course he did not. He just turned his face to the Lord. Faith has only to do with the way you turn your face, or to whom! It has to do with our posture toward God.

Do you think we can really accept that kind of theology? That is the theology that there is no special saving power in Jesus' crucifixion in itself. Jesus did not say it was a payment for our sins. He said it was just a symbol like the snake in the desert. Can you believe that the cross only stands for the fact that God is a God who intends to save us, all of us—and God will go to any lengths to get that across to us! God arranged for a symbol in the middle of history to demonstrate that. So when you and I look at that symbol its redemptive power is in the fact that it reminds us that God intends to save us. Believing that we can trust God for that is the faith that opens us to receive God's salvation—to believe and accept God's radical grace. All the mechanics of the cross as the payment for sin are out the window if we take Jesus seriously.

God gave to Moses and the Israelites a symbol and its signal that God intends to save us all. That symbol was sufficiently articulate and attention-getting to communicate the message to them in that ancient moment. The meaning of that symbol got lost in the detritus of history. So God strategized to set a symbol in the middle of history that no one could ever forget. There upon a blood-spattered Roman cross hung God's self, that is, a man with a life full of God! Now we cannot get that image out of our minds and hearts. We cannot reason it out, we cannot puke it out, we cannot ignore it out, we cannot neglect it out, and we cannot get it out. We cannot get around it, past it, behind it, beyond it, over it, or under it. There it stands in the middle of history, the hanging Galilean. We can only go through it to God!

I think this way of looking at things is directly related to Paul's remark that in the end "every eye shall see him, every knee shall bow, of things in heaven and things in earth and of things under the earth (*Sheol*, death), and every tongue shall confess that Christ is Lord to the glory of God the

Father" (Rom 14:11; Phil 2:10–11). When we die, we shall all stand before God. If we think to ourselves, "Oh, what will happen to me now?" we shall immediately see Christ Jesus standing there, and we shall all respond as Thomas did, "My Lord and My God!"

That is, when you die you will see Jesus. Then you will remember, "Ah, I recognize him! There is the symbol. God intends nothing but my healing and salvation. That is what God is like. I am free at last! I am free at last! Thank God Almighty, I am free at last!" Every human person will be saved and free at last.

This is a very interesting and unusual theology Jesus is revealing here. I think it is the heart of Christianity. It is our true Christian hope! Our central saving certainty! Our only chance!

Amen. So let it Be!

SERMON TWENTY TWO

The Minister's Mandate, the Congregation's Call

—Matthew 16:13b–18b

> The church is built on a rock.
>
> — MATTHEW 16:18

THE MINISTER'S MANDATE AND the congregation's call are the two essential factors in God's business in the Christian movement. God's work is set forth in Jesus' words, "I will build my church and the gates of hell shall not stand up against it" (Matt 16:18b). God has been building his church for twenty centuries. These have not been uniformly bright times for the church. These twenty centuries of the church's history have been fraught with the horrors of abuse, immorality, war, and genocide perpetrated in God's name. We have suffered conflict over doctrine and over liturgy. That conflict often led to persecution and the murder of innocent people and strife over power and authority.

The history of this church that God has been building has been marked in every century by perfidy in leadership, hostile division, hatred, and corruption. One side of the history of the church is a story of evil, barbarism, and tragedy. Moreover, that continues to the recent sexual abuse of children by priests and the latest moral and financial scandals in the Vatican. Who would want to be a member of such an institution, community, organism, or organization? Who would want to be a part of God's enterprise with a history like that? Much of the time the church has been less Christian than the secular world of disinterested folks and unbelievers.

Well, that is the human side of the church of Jesus Christ our Lord. Then there is the other side. No force or community in the history of the world has done so much as the church has, or been so effective in creating human idealism and values, inspiring tenderness for and care of the needy, and producing beauty in human character and in the arts. In the best and worst of times the church has been the community of faith, the institution preaching and enacting God's grace, and the organization militating for goodness. I am still for the church—in spite of herself. We are the fellowship of the faithful, the community of the committed, those who gather because we rejoice to hear the word of God proclaimed. We come together to celebrate God's unconditional forgiveness of all humans.

The notable English historian Arnold Toynbee once said that writers and professors of history often think that history is the record of the battles won or lost, the parliaments deliberating, the legislation enacted, and the actions of presidents, kings, and generals. Historians are oriented on the dates and times of major changes in the course of politics, societies, and cultures. Toynbee advised that we should not ever think that such things constitute history. Those are merely the flotsam and jetsam that float down the surface of the stream of history and in the end they are all relatively irrelevant and are washed away.

History, said Toynbee, is the abundant, colorful, and playful life that goes on down in the depths of the stream of history and that is unfolding on the banks of that rapidly flowing river. There people are singing and dancing, loving and making love, conceiving and bearing children, baptizing and rearing their children with joy and faith, and burying their dead with dignity. That is history, Toynbee declared. So it is with the church. It is not the humanness of the church's history which is the crucial reality and the surprising fact. It is the healing and redeeming presence of the church in history—despite its humanness—that is the surprise, the crucial fact, and the gift to the world.

Blaise Pascal, a famous early modern philosopher and theologian, declared that there is sure evidence for the divine nature of this human institution we call the church. That evidence lies in the church's continued existence through all these centuries despite its incredibly human and dysfunctional leadership. Who would want to be a member of this human, yet divine, institution and community? We would! We are the company of the committed. We are here to say that we are ready to take up together my minister's mandate and your congregation's call.

Jesus said, "I will build my church!" He did not say, *You go and build my church*. On the rock of Peter's confession of faith, "You are the Christ," God will build the church in this place. That means the growth of the church in depth and size is God's business, but God will be pleased to have us on board so we will be part of the solution instead of just part of the problem. The church will flourish here *with* us or *in spite of* us, depending upon how effectively I take up my mandate and you take up your call. We are not inherently necessary to this business of God building the church, but God invites us to be part of it. If we want to have meaningful and useful lives, it is useful for us to get on board God's program of grace.

So today we respond together to God's invitation. How shall we do that? Well I have a plan. The plan is to concentrate upon the deepening of personal spirituality in our congregation. I am persuaded that if we concentrate upon deepening and expanding our personal spirituality all the questions regarding the flourishing of the church will take care of themselves quite naturally.

The size of the church in numbers is not a central issue in God's building God's church but the depth and breadth of spirituality certainly is. Of course, numbers are important in the sense that there are many folk in our community who are hungering for our ministry of God's grace and the consolations of deepened spirituality. Moreover, as we endeavor to expand our work to embrace our community we need more hands and hearts to provide the energy, time, and money to support the expanding ministry. I believe that expansion will happen if we work on what it means to cultivate a deep spirituality.

My plan is to build an intimate fellowship with all of you by meeting with each of you on a regular and continuing basis. Moreover, when we meet to speak together, we will not talk of the weather. We will talk about your soul. If that sounds scary, fear not, because it is quite easy to speak of the things of the spirit, even of your own spirit in a non-scary, indeed, in a gratifying way.

If this sounds like an idealistic vision, let me mention a passage in Proverbs 29:18, "Where there is no vision the people perish." I invite you to the grand Christian vision described in Jesus' final pastoral prayer in John 17:11–19, "Holy Father, protect your church by the power of your name, so that they may be one as we are one. My prayer is not that you take them out of this world but that you protect them from the power of evil. Make them holy by your truth. Your word is truth. As you sent me into the world, so I send them into the world. For them I make myself holy that they too may be made holy."

Notice that Jesus declares that God should protect the church by the power of God's name. Proverbs 18:10 says, "The name of Yahweh is a strong tower, the righteous run into it and are safe." The name, Yahweh, is God's covenant name. It means, "I will always be for you what I have always been for you!" God's faithfulness to us in spite of ourselves is a strong tower. We cannot sin ourselves out of God's grace nor squirm out of God's long embrace.

With the likes of us, God will build his church here. We can be part of it or lose out on it. That is our choice regarding our mandate and call. I have nothing to prove here but the declaration of God's forgiving grace. Where Jesus is confessed as the Christ of God, the church is in the process of developing. I am for the church. It is the only institution that still *intends* to hold out for decency, truth, and righteousness at all cost. Let us do this work together in the assurances of God's name.

Amen. So let it Be!

SERMON TWENTY THREE

Christian Olympics
—Hebrews 12:1–2a

> Run the race with perseverance.
> —Hebrews 12:1c

DEEPENING AND BROADENING OUR spirituality is essential for good psychological and spiritual health. However, that does not mean devaluing the material world that is rich with God's blessings to us. It means instead a shift of the focus of life away from preoccupation with the superficial and trivializing effects of *things* and toward living life with the sense of being before the face of God. In that sense our ministry as pastor and people is *a way of life*.

You may feel like saying, "Pastor, it is all good and well for you to talk about ministry as our way of life. You get paid to make ministry your way of life. We have to work for a living." Well that is true, in a certain way, but that is also beside the point that I am making. I could slide by with doing a good job of administration, get to most of the meetings on time, conduct a decent liturgy on Sunday, and the like. I could get away with that. Some ministers do. I would look then pretty much like those. However, that is not what I do. I work hard in trying to produce profound preaching and pastoring, not because it is my job but because it is my way of being me. I would not get caught dead doing less. It would just not be me. There would be no gratification in it for me or any meaningful help in it for you.

This matter of ministry for me is about the extent of my devotion and the style of my sense of calling. It is for me a way of life. So is it with you. Being a Christian is doing your "working for a living," your daily life and love, as a life of consciously dedicated devotion. I do not mean that life needs to be something somber and long-faced. I think ministry is often hilarious, delightful, and joyful. There are constant unexpected twists and turns, some sadness and heavy burdens, but on the whole it is a remarkably gratifying journey. Being a Christian means living your daily life and doing your daily loving consciously and intentionally *before God's face*. It is really enjoyable to live the life of ministering God's forgiving grace with a sense of doing it all the time in God's presence.

So Paul and the author of the Hebrews say that we have a race to run, a race before God and all God's people. The Bible says we have a great cloud of witnesses before whom we run. Hebrews has a long list of all the heroes of faith—all those on earth and in heaven who have gone before us in this determined life of articulating and enacting God's radical and unconditional grace to everybody in the world, wherever we happen to be at any given moment..

I decided at the age of seven that this was my race. I thank God that the call to ministry for me was so clear and unequivocal right from that beginning moment. It was a bright sunny August day and I was standing outside the horse barn door smelling the horse manure and sensing all the sensations of farm life. The illumination came to me with utter clarity. It reminds me of the famous Bulgarian discus thrower whose biography I once read.

This young lad at age twelve was taken with his classmates to a museum during the Communist era. There he saw a marvelous Greek vase excavated by an archaeologist somewhere near where he lived. The vase was decorated with classic pictures depicting scenes from the ancient Olympics. He saw the ancient discus thrower. From that moment he decided that was for him. He began immediately to practice, determined to equip himself as a heroic athlete, like the one he had seen on the vase.

As he continued his quest to cultivate a great skill in discus-throwing he learned of the ancient Olympics and of the new Olympics held in our day. He set his face steadfastly to enter the Olympics and to win. Unfortunately, he was not selected by the Communist government to become a professional discus thrower and train with official help and support. So, despite the fact that he had to work for a living, he continued his avocation as a dedicated discus-thrower. He made a living as a teacher and that made it possible for him to teach himself to be the best discus thrower in the land.

His vocation kept him alive. His avocation became his way of life. Disciplined, diligent, enduring, and self-motivated, he followed this costly quest. Eventually the day came when it was clear to everyone that he was the obvious choice from all Bulgaria to represent the country in the Olympic Games. He had kept alive the anticipation that one day he would be surrounded by the great cloud of witnesses and so he ran with patience this race set before him. He made his avocation his way of life and he won the gold. Christian life in ministry, whether a minister's mandate or a congregation's call is just like that. Regardless of how you work for a living, living life before the face of God means that in everything you do you are in ministry, regardless of your job. Our avocation is our calling. That is the thing.

Every year the Olympics start over. In 2004 the Olympics returned to Athens near where they began three thousand years ago. For the grand and ancient city of Athens this has been a long and demanding race. Six years seeking the permission to invite the Olympics to its historic metropolis and six years preparing the city for the spectacular events. An Olympic-sized endeavor in itself! Many did not believe that Athens could pull it off. The American media underrated that city every day from every point of view, decrying the fact that Athens would never be able to do it right or get ready in time. That commentary demonstrated the consummate irrelevance and erroneousness of American broadcast media. It said nothing truthful about Athens' Olympic race against time, terrorism, and fiscal challenges.

Self-motivated, disciplined, diligent, patient, enduring in its focus, the city faced the costly risks and achieved the goal successfully. Committed at all costs, surrounded by the whole world as a great cloud of witnesses, she has run with patience the race set before her, throwing aside all encumbrances and the burdens which always beset such an enterprise, she looked to the ideal and the goal, not to public opinion. She did not play to the bleachers but to the task, and she won through.

When Hebrews was written, the Olympics were already six hundred to one thousand years old and going strong. It is not surprising, therefore, that the Bible uses the metaphor of the Olympic competitions, and in doing so links it with the minister's mandate and the congregation's call to ministry. The author of this epistle and of the Pauline epistles both use that metaphor. They imagine the Olympics as the metaphor of the Christian life. They envision life before the face of God as a Christian Olympics.

Our text is built around that metaphor: *Seeing that we are surrounded by so great a cloud of witnesses (the dedicated believers on earth and in heaven—heroes of faith) let us throw aside all the baggage and the sin which so easily besets us (everything which would distract and obstruct our concentration) and let us run with patience the race that is set before us, looking to Jesus, the author and completer of our odyssey of faith* . . . . Paul declared to the Corinthian congregation (1Cor. 9:26), "I do not run uncertainly or as one who is merely beating the air with his arms . . .But I run so that you may be blameless and harmless, the children of God, without rebuke amidst this corrupt and perverse generation, among whom you [*who run life as a Christian Olympics*] shine as lights in the world, holding forth the word of life; that I may not have run in vain, nor labored in vain" (Phil 2:15-16).

So we run together for the next weeks or months or years. We are not going to run uncertainly, nor as those who are merely beating the air, or spinning our wheels, as we say in our day. We run together as those who are well aware of the fact that a great crowd of the heroes of faith have gone before us in this enterprise of the kingdom—the great community of faith on earth and in heaven who have ministered before us.

We run with patience, that is, with dogged devotion to every task, menial or heroic, manual or intellectual, practical or theoretical, doing each as though it is as important to the whole work as preaching on Sunday. In this manner and style let us run the race that is set before us. It is interesting that the author of this text uses that language. Obviously he means to imply that he did not choose this race. It was set before him. He was appointed to it. It was not just his job. It was his vocation. That is the old Latin word for one's calling. Let us run with patience the race to which we have all been called. Running with patience in this case means running with unflagging endurance.

Paul says we run looking to Jesus. That is, we run the race in his name and spirit, not playing to the bleachers, not for our own power and glory, but running as he ran. Our spiritual jackets have his endorsement on them instead of Dunham's or Dick's Sporting Goods. Now that does not mean that we run this race with Jesus as our example. That would be a trivialization of this race. He ran his race and we must run ours. In the nineteenth century there was a lot of emphasis upon Jesus as our example. You have all read the rather famous book *In His Steps*, by Charles Monroe Sheldon, which set forth that notion. But that is the wrong idea. Jesus is not our example. He lived in the first century in a radically different culture from ours and we live in the twenty-first century. He had to do his thing in that setting and we have to live our lives before the face of God in our setting.

Some of the things Jesus said and did make absolutely no sense in terms of the imperatives of our age. They did not even make sense in terms of the requirements of his age. He said we should all be poverty stricken mendicants who begged for our livelihood while we went from door-to-door preaching. His idea failed then and it would fail now. In Mark 8 the disciples came back to him and said, *It does not work. The mission is a bust.* So Jesus began to change his approach and tried to find a more successful method, but he just got himself into more and more political trouble, until he provoked the authorities by tearing up the temple, so they killed him.

Jesus is not our example. He is our paradigm. Do you know the difference between an example and a paradigm? Well, I think I do, so let me try to set that out as clearly as I can. If you wanted to tell someone how coal cars operate in a coal mine, you might say, "Well, you know what a train looks like and how it operates by running with special wheels on two iron tracks. That is what a coal car in a coal mine is like. The train is an example of such a coal car." People would immediately envision what you meant. They would know that there is a difference between a train and a coal car, but they would see in their mind's eye how remarkably they were alike.

Now, if you were to try to explain to someone the similarity and difference of a freight train and interstate freight trucks, you would say that they are alike in that they fit into the same category as interstate freight haulers. They are also very different. They are really not alike at all. Neither is an example of the other. But they fit into the same paradigm, the same category: interstate freight-haulers. Jesus is our paradigm. We are called to do in our day the kind of thing he was trying to work out in his day, namely, living his life in very life-changing ways before the face of God, so as to do enormous temporal and eternal good for all those around him that he could touch.

Jesus constantly badgered the authorities because he saw that a social-political change was necessary in order to create a setting for spiritual change. I am not sure he was right about that. By the time that Paul wrote his letters a generation later, he was already discerning the difference in the setting, so he enjoins, "Let every person be subject to the governmental powers for there are no powers but from God and the powers that be are ordained by God" (Rom 13:1). For Paul, Jesus was not an example but a categorical paradigm. So he is for us. Jesus would not back down from his claim that God's grace is totally forgiving for all humans and he behaved like he meant it. Existing as a paradigm of divine grace in the world was his mode. That is also our paradigm. We need to find the effective ways of enacting that in the 21st century.

So we will run our race here together, aware of the witnesses, throwing aside distractions, advancing with patience, looking to Jesus who is the source and consummation of our faith, its author and finisher. We will depend heavily on leaders, helpers, and participants in our ministry. We need all of them equally. Without participants there is no work for leaders and helpers. Without helpers and participants there is no one to lead. Without leaders the good that we would do we will not, and the failures we do not want we will get. We need each other, each in his and her calling in this race. Each is equally crucial for this vocation in ministry and Christian life.

We are not laggards, but laborers together. We are spiritual athletes in this Christian Olympics. If you are going to be a spiritual athlete you must not miss the practices. Your presence is a crucial part of the performance. *Remember that Christian life is not a spectator sport.*

Amen. So let it Be!

SERMON TWENTY FOUR

The Empty God
—Philippians 2:5–11

> He emptied himself and took on the form of a servant.
> —PHILIPPIANS 2:7

A GREAT DEAL OF scholarship has been invested over the last 150 years into discovering what the real Jesus was like and who he really was. I myself have spent sixty years on exactly that issue. Lately, scholars have come nearer than ever to a crisp and clear understanding of that man from first century Galilee. While each scholar who has attempted to write a recent narrative describing Jesus has quite a different perspective on the matter, one thing is very certain. It is the fact that Paul was right when he wrote about thirty or forty years after Jesus' death that God had given Jesus a name that is above every name, that at the name of Jesus every knee should bow (Rom 14:11, Phil 2:10). This has become a practical fact. Almost everywhere in the world humans have come to see his name as being above every name.

The reason for this fact is the inherent appeal in Jesus' words and in his manner of handling people. Paul described it graphically and the gospels tell the unfolding story of why Paul said what he said. Paul declared that

Jesus did not consider being equal with God as a thing to be held on to. He emptied himself of all his divine prerogatives and took upon himself the form of a servant, to be born as a human being. Being thus found in the form of a human, he humbled himself in obedience to a destiny of suffering and death—indeed, a crucifixion, thus acquiring the notability of a name that is remembered better than every other name.

The gospels tell us that this was no smooth trip for Jesus Christ. We hear him implore God, "Let this cup pass from me!" We hear him cry in desperation, "My God, My God, why have you forsaken me?" (Mark 14:36, 15:34).

Recently I joined the local Jewish community at worship in their synagogue. While we were there I noticed this prayer in the Jewish Prayer Book:

> If I am not for me, who will be?
> If I do not seek my own, who will?
> If not now, when?

That sentiment is exactly opposite from the mind of Christ! If that were the mind of Christ, his name would not be above every name, because that Jewish prayer is simply a very ordinary form of the narcissism that is ruining American society and culture. Moreover, that narcissistic attitude from the Jewish Prayer Book is the thing that has turned Israel into the tail that destructively wags the entire geopolitical dog today. Paul enjoins us instead to have the mind in us that was in Jesus Christ (Phil 2:5), namely, to empty ourselves of our own prerogatives and take up the role of servant of all. In our world and in this country we are free to be anything we want to be, but if we want to claim to be Christians, Paul asserts that it means we must have the mind of Christ in us.

Paul does not leave us wondering what he means by having the mind of Christ or taking up the role of a servant. He uses such phrases as being in full accord with one another, having the same love in us as Christ had, allowing no room for selfishness or narcissism, holding the interests of others before our own interests, loving our neighbors as instinctively as we seek the welfare and survival of ourselves, and having that humility which prefers others before ourselves. Now we know what he means by Christ and Christians emptying ourselves of our own prerogatives.

Paul had a clear sense of what outcome this would produce. Christ is exalted around the world because none of us can forget that blood-spattered Roman cross poking its head up on that wind-swept Judean hill. Mel Gibson's film, *The Passion of Christ,* has been severely criticized for being excessively violent and sadistic. I doubt that one can portray the real suffering of that man from Nazareth in any way that would even begin to tell the wretched story of how much he suffered. If one can criticize that movie, it surely cannot be for being too vivid in portraying Christ's ordeal. "My God, My God, why have *you forsaken* me?" (Mark 15:34).

"Every knee should bow, in heaven and on earth and under the earth, and every tongue should confess that Jesus Christ is Lord, to the glory of God the Father," says Paul, quite prophetically (Rom 14:11, Phil 2:10–11).

The first great Christian theologian after Paul was Irenaeus of Lyons. His theological model was not an atonement model centered on the cross of Christ as payment for our sins. His was a creation theology in which he saw the first Adam as distorting God's original design by his disobedience; God undertaking in grace to embrace the whole human race in God's love anyway and Christ as the second Adam coming to fulfill the original design of God for the whole creation by his grace-filled way of cherishing people. The whole divine economy is like an envelope which contains creation, sustaining and guiding providence, and salvation. The entire package, begun in creation, is completed in Christ's courageous willingness to stand for God's truth, grace, and love against all odds, and never back down. "Having loved his own he loved them unto the end, even the death on the cross" (John 13:1).

In Irenaeus's model Christ's obedience cancels out Adam's disobedience and restores God's original design for all things, namely, a free, forgiven, healed world of joyful and wholesome spirituality. All fear, guilt, and shame that is weighing us down is cancelled out. Thus the death on the cross is not some transcendent divine atonement design, but rather a horrible accident of history; which, nonetheless demonstrates how far God and God's unique son will go to get across the message of divine truth, grace, mercy, and love. Jesus' ordeal demonstrates how important it is to stand for that. The cross epitomizes a demonstration theology, not an atonement theology. Jesus calls all of us in this complex and painful world to that courageous stance.

So Irenaeus's perception of God's total economy for his created world is one in which that whole divine design is completed, not in the cross, but in humanity restored to the divinely intended status of having in us the mind of Christ. This was Irenaeus's and Paul's notion of God's shalom for God's world. It reflected the very nature of Jesus Christ, who emptied himself of all his heavenly prerogatives so that as a man among men he might save us all by demonstrating the costly but critical nature of the authentic mindset of saving grace and forgiveness for everyone, for everything, for evermore.

Amen. So let it Be!

SERMON TWENTY FIVE

Spirituality Right Side Up
—Ephesians 2:4–10

> By grace we are saved . . . a gift of God, for we are God's workmanship, created in Christ Jesus for good works, which God prepared beforehand that we should walk in them.
>
> — Ephesians 2:8, 2:10

WE GENERALLY BELIEVE THAT if we behave ourselves God will love us and if we misbehave we endanger our relationship with God. That is a lie. Things do not work that way. Fortunately the world is not wired that way. That logic is contrary to the Bible. Of course, it seems so intuitively correct, because we know very well that if we behave ourselves as children, Mother smiles. If we do not behave ourselves as children bad things happen. It is easy for us to extrapolate from that experience an equation that we apply to our own spirituality and to our own relationship with God. Paul's whole point in Ephesians is to describe in a very operational way how this business of our encounter and interaction with God really works. He says that it does not work the way the Pharisees thought it worked. It works the way Jesus claimed it works.

The Pharisees were sure that if you got people to behave correctly and follow their 613 religious regulations, people would automatically and progressively get a change of heart. Their inner world would line up with their obedient behavior. In our day this method is called *brainwashing*: to get externally forced behavior to reshape the inner code of a person's life. B. F. Skinner called it the theory and practice of behaviorism. Ivan Pavlov called it classic conditioning.

Jesus' debate with the Pharisees was a debate about Jesus' claim that you cannot start with an external system, impose it on people, and get a change of the heart. Change needs to start in the spirit and then you may expect that the external behavior of that person will line up with the internal change. Paul extrapolated from that the essential perspective that he thought was true Christianity, true spirituality right side up. Paul explained that the only manner in which you can get change in the heart is by *surprising it into existence*. We need to be surprised with the announcement that God has removed from the equation of our relationship with God everything that has to do with human fear, guilt, and shame. You cannot get there by commanding right behavior.

Now it is interesting that Paul says that the entire objective of God in history and with you and me is to get us to produce good works. That sounds like what the church was busy with for twenty centuries. It sounds like what the Pharisees thought it was all about. It is easy to forget that Paul introduced that very notion with the most radical statement of grace that appears anywhere in the Bible. "By grace you are saved, through faith, and that not of yourselves; it is a gift of God, not of works, lest anyone should boast" (Eph 2:8). Then he followed that with the observation, "We are created in Christ Jesus for good works" (Eph 2:10). Thus the whole point of God coming to us in Christ, and announcing that fear, guilt, and shame do not count, is to empower us for doing God's work in the world, with none of our energy distracted or wasted on our flaws and failures.

The only thing that counts is being committed to Christ and accepting the freedom and relief of being radically forgiven in advance. Then you do not even have to consider the question of your behavior, except to realize that God's whole purpose for you is that your life should be filled with good works. Good works means good works like Jesus did: feeding the hungry, caring for the sick, raising the dead, healing the lepers, giving sight to the blind, filling the lost and the lonely with the spirit of Christ's love, filling the world with the experience of the presence and power of the Divine Spirit.

Paul caught the truth of that, and so he got the spirituality right side up. He caught it like an infection, it filled his whole life. It permeated everything he said and did. It permeated his motivation to spend his life spreading this radical good news. He abandoned himself to explaining how the God/human interaction works operationally. He saw God in uncalculating grace forgiving everybody without consideration of the nature or seriousness of their dysfunction. Grace turns humans loose to realize that our only agenda is to do good. Forgiveness frees all our psychic energy to invest it in spiritual growth, and in behavior that helps and heals our flawed and fractured world.

In my ministry I have not emphasized the Christian calling to do good work as much as I have emphasized our freedom in God's grace. It is so much more difficult for people to get a grasp on the realty of grace. All of us humans have difficulty in really entrusting ourselves to this incredible announcement that our behavior does not count in the equation of our relationship with God. I have emphasized that if we have really gotten that word we will turn our faces toward God and declare that we want to be God's kind of people. Then the good work comes by itself. If we really accept and believe that God takes us as we are, whether we are good or bad—that God loves us absolutely, and will not let us go—we will be really empowered to actually become and perform what God genuinely intends for us to be and do. God intends us to be people who are just churning out the good works—a life full of world-changing and life-changing helpfulness and healing behavior.

Remember the life of Saint Augustine. He lived for about thirty-five years as the most wretched kind of profligate person you can imagine. Any evil thing you think a human can do he was busy doing for thirty-five years. Then he was miraculously converted. He became as crazy in the exaggeration of his Christianity as he had in his paganism. His sins and iniquities had a lot to do with sexual misbehavior and when he was converted to Christianity he wanted to get rid of sex all together. Neither one of those is a good idea, but the point is that he got the central message of faith. If you read his *Confessions*, you can notice that he got the point that, despite those thirty-five years of terrible life, he was clean and free, simply by the announcement in scripture that God forgave him unconditionally. Thereafter, he wanted more and more intensely to find out how to be God's kind of person, operationally.

By Grace Alone

God forgave him for a specific reason. God did not want him wasting his energy any longer on evil behavior, but neither did he want him wasting his energy any longer on being fearful, guilty, or shameful about it. God wanted to get rid of that. God wanted to remove that from God's equation and ours. God wants to set us on a course on which we are no longer wasting any part of our time, focus, fervor, function, enthusiasm, or energy on fear, guilt, and shame, anxiety, distraction, or sorrow, but only on growing in grace and producing good works that heal lives and institutions in God's needy world.

Have you ever seen one of those converts who has spent long years in wretched self-defeating behavior, perhaps as an alcoholic or criminal? Then he or she is converted and spends the next twenty years of life bewailing the sinfulness of the past and continuing to get a lot of attention out of celebrating the grief of guilt, shame, and fear. I am sure you remember that it makes you want to say, "Your new Christian life is about as narcissistic as your old wicked one was. You are still completely self-preoccupied. Formerly you were self-preoccupied in the indulgence of bad habits, and now you are self-preoccupied in wasting time and energy on fear, guilt, and shame." All the while God is saying, "That is not part of the equation. I want you out of that so you can get on with a life full of growth and ministry. You were meant for a life full of good works, full of wholesome activity that makes a constructive difference in the lives of needy or suffering persons and cultures. Do not spend your life on negative spiritual narcissism that exhausts you of all good things."

When I was a child we had members in our church who were from a very conservative Dutch Reformed background. They would not come to the Lords Supper because they were sure that they were not good enough for it. They spent their entire lives believing, thinking, and arguing about how they were not good enough. They could just as well have given that up and come to the table and had fun being Christians because that is what God wants. Wasting ourselves on fear, guilt, and shame is a terrible thing. It's an evil thing because it refuses to really take seriously the radical nature of the Christian gospel—this good news about forgiving grace.

Luther was converted from medieval Catholic legalism in which he was sure that he had to go through all sorts of performances to make certain that God was not genuinely ticked off at him. Luther was not narcissistic in his spirituality. He was neurotic. He was afraid of everything. He felt guilty about everything. He was ashamed of everything. Then one day

Spirituality Right Side Up

he saw the passage in Ephesians 2 and he realized he was set free. He went out, as it were, and changed the world for God. He took all of his neurotic energy and invested it in a radical sense of freedom. He trusted the Lord for it. He trusted God that as radical as God's grace is, so radical was Luther's freedom, and that he could not sin himself out of God's grace. So he went full throttle to do the things that made a difference for the kingdom; teaching, studying, and creating congregations of caring people.

Psalm 37:3 says it all comes down to one thing: "trust in the Lord and do good." Trust the Lord that God is going to handle all the stuff that you might have to worry about. You just get on with doing good things that change the world and make a big difference for people who need our help.

When I was at the worst moment in my life, when I thought everything was going down the tube and I could not even sleep, God gave me that verse, "Trust in the Lord and do good," and it changed my life. It set me on a high road in which I could leave all the anguish to God, and just go on doing God's thing. That is what life is all about, it seems to me. We are created in Christ Jesus for good works. That is God's purpose with us. If we constantly spend our energy on fear, guilt, and shame, we do not have the clear head to get on with constructive work. If we cannot quite accept the radical nature of God's grace, then we simply do not have the recourses fully available for doing the good work that God needs to have done.

"By grace you have been saved, through faith, and that not of yourselves; it is a gift of God, not of works lest you should boast . . . . We are created in Christ Jesus for good works, which God prepared beforehand, to be our way of life" (Eph 2:8, 2:10)

The Good Samaritan found a fellow suffering, picked him up, got him healed, and paid the medical bill (Luke 10:30–37). There were a lot of wonderful religionists around who did not do that. A priest and a Levite saw the wounded man lying there in the ditch bleeding to death. The priest or pastor said, "I am too busy, I have to make my 9:00 Bible class at church. Besides, if I try to help him I will get my new preaching suit bloody and filthy." So he left the man in the ditch and passed by as far on the other side of the road as he could safely walk. The Levite or Clerk of Session said, "The poor guy is impure because he has been violated and is bleeding and I am on my way to the special session meeting and the worship service. I cannot take the time and delay my rush to church. I am running late already and I must set the example of being on time for my sacred duties. If I am not exemplary in this everyone will start coming late and chaos will reign," so he left the man to die. In the back of his mind was the litany: "The fellow probably had it coming. Who knows what kind of company this low-class character keeps? In any case it looks like he is a goner." And he abandoned the dying man.

Only the Samaritan who happened along paid attention to this suffering Jew. Samaritans were considered by the Jews to be impure. They were a mixed breed, despised by God's good upper-class churchmen, pure-blood Jews. They viewed a Samaritan as inferior. Well this regular sort of guy, the Samaritan, who was not religious at all, and was accustomed to feeling the raw side of life, stopped for the bleeding man. Only the Samaritan who did not have any religious obligations and meetings to attend! Only the Samaritan, who himself could imagine having been assaulted, neglected, and thrown aside by all the grand people of God and the religious institutions. Only he picked up the wounded man, took him to a hospital, paid the bill, and got him well.

By grace we are saved, and thereby God has created us in Christ Jesus for good works. If you have heard the gospel of radical grace then get on with the business that comes after that good news—the business for which we were created in Christ Jesus—the business of being God's kind or persons.

Amen. So let it Be!

SERMON TWENTY SIX

Spirituality Upside Down and Inside Out

—James

> Abraham believed God and it was counted to him for righteousness. So you see that he was justified by works.
>
> — JAMES 2:22–24

"SHOW ME YOUR FAITH without your deeds and I will show you my faith by my good deeds" (Jas 2:18). I have noticed in sixty years of ministry that there are two things that scare the daylights out of most Christians. The first is for me to say that I do not believe that there is a devil. It is amazing how urgently some Christians need to believe in a devil. Sometimes I think the non-existent devil is more palpably real to them than God. The second is for me to say that God's grace is so absolutely radical that we are saved in spite of ourselves in every case, and not because of anything that we can do, even anything in the form of correct believing.

The Epistle of James had a very difficult time getting approved as part of the Bible. The decision to include it was made at the Council of Nicaea in

325 CE, but there was a long and vigorous debate about whether James was really a book with a proper Christian theme and outlook. Twelve hundred years later the Protestant Reformers once again took up the question of whether James was a proper biblical book. Luther was sure that it should be thrown out and in fact did ignore it completely in his entire ministry. He said that it was an epistle of straw, worthless, and to be discarded. There are good reasons why this kind of a debate took place with regard to the book of James. Some other books also had similar difficulty getting into the biblical canon, but James had the toughest time and the reason is that James is extremely confused in its line of argument. It is psychologically confused, literarily confused, and theologically confused. James has his spirituality inside out and upside down. It is really a kind of Old Testament book in the New Testament.

The Epistle of James represents the earliest expression of the Christian church. James was the brother of Jesus and he ran the church in Jerusalem which developed around Jesus' family. They believed that Jesus was a human being and a great teacher. They denied the virgin birth and contested the ideas of the Greek speaking Jewish church established by Peter. Paul established the church of Greek speaking Gentiles. James' church in Jerusalem lasted about two generations and died out. Remnants of its emphasis were preserved in what later came to be known as the Syrian Church in the northeast part of the Christian world.

James's *psychological* confusion starts out pretty early in the text of his Epistle. In 2:17 he says "Faith by itself, if it is not expressed in godly work, is dead." In that statement James is making what is essentially a patently untrue remark. It is not the case that faith without works is dead. He should never have said that. The truth is that it may be very much alive. That is, faith is the sort of thing that even if it is a very minute experience of trust in God, it is nonetheless true faith and saving faith.

Jesus himself specifically said that if you have faith as small as a mustard seed it is saving faith. Mustard seed is about the smallest seed that you can actually see without a microscope. "If you have faith as small as a mustard seed, you can move mountains" (Matt 17:20b). It is not the productivity of the faith. It is the quality of trust that connects us in a saving way to God. Faith may, for example, be unfruitful in a person's life at any given moment simply because it is immature or uninformed or timid or not actualized. People may be at one of many different locations in the process of the Christian pilgrimage and in the process of Christian development. So

Spirituality Upside Down and Inside Out

James is blatantly wrong. What he says in the Bible is untrue. Faith without works is not *necessarily* dead.

Then in 2:19 he says, "You believe in the one true God, so do the demons. They believe and tremble." Well that's a bad trick. He should never have gotten away with that. He is using the word *believe* in two different ways in that one verse. He is using it first in the meaning of trust in God—true faith. When we say, "I believe in God," we mean "I trust in God, I long for God, I reach out to God, I know that God has embraced me." That is how I believe and that is how the Christians believed to whom James wrote his epistle.

Then in the second case he says that the demons also believe—and tremble. He is saying that the demons acknowledge the existence of God. You and I are smart enough to realize that now he is talking a different language. To believe in God for our salvation is one thing. To acknowledge the existence of God is something altogether different and does not imply faith, trust, or wholesome relationship with God in the first sense James used it. James' argument is specious and deceptive. To know and trust God is a very different thing than to know about or acknowledge the existence of God.

It is altogether different to say, on the one hand, "I believe that God exists" and then the other hand to say, "I believe in God in the sense that I profoundly trust in and love God." Trying to pull that manipulative trick is like the difference between the philosophical statement, "I know about God," and the faith statement, "I know God and am deeply devoted to God." Unless he was really dumb, James was intentionally tricking and deceiving us. He was intentionally using psychological manipulation. He should not be allowed to do that.

From there, James goes on to *literary* confusion. Beginning in 2:20, he says a number of things in which he asks the question, "Do you want to be shown, you senseless person, that faith apart from works is barren? Was not our ancestor Abraham justified by works when he offered his son, Isaac, on the altar? You see that faith was active along with his works and faith was brought to completion by his works. Thus the scripture was fulfilled when it says, 'Abraham believed God and it was reckoned to him as righteousness and he was called a friend of God.' You see that a person is justified by works and not by faith alone."

James has just proven that Abraham was justified by his faith, not by his works, and then he draws the opposite conclusion. It is literary confusion. Notice his argument. Do you believe in the one true God? Do you believe that faith without works is fruitful and is real faith? Do you believe that Abraham was justified by his works when the scripture plainly says it was by his faith that he was justified? Then he concludes that Abraham was justified by his works.

James twists the logic and the symmetry here by arbitrarily drawing the very opposite conclusion than he has just proven. If you go on to 2:26 he says, "As the body without the spirit is dead, so faith without works is dead." James is again twisting the logic and the symmetry and manipulating the conclusion and manipulating us, his audience. What he should have said is this, "As the body without the spirit is dead, so deeds (which are the material counterpart of the palpable body) without faith (which is the counterpart of vitality and spirituality) are dead." As the body without the spirit is dead, so deeds without faith are dead. But he says "so faith without deeds is dead." How absurd! He turns the argument upside down with no justification for it and so intentionally manipulates the conclusion and his audience.

Let us go on to his *theological* confusion. In 2:14 he asks "What good is it my brothers and sisters if you say that you have faith, but do not have works? Can faith save you?" Now the answer to that question in Paul's epistles and the answer to that question in the Old Testament is, "Yes, faith can save you all by itself." As a matter of fact, it's the only thing that does save you. Paul says, "By grace are you saved through faith and that not of yourselves, it is a gift of God, not of works lest anyone should boast that he or she has saved himself by doing good" (Eph 2:8–9).

Isaiah 64:6 tells us "All our righteousness and all the good we do are as used menstrual rags—worthless. To be disposed of and burned—useless." In 2:20–24, James uses terms like "justified by deeds" and so forth. Well then what of the cross? Then what of the Eucharist? Incidentally, neither one of those two important factors in the gospels and in Paul's epistles appears anywhere in James.

So here we have a book in the Bible that is all mixed up and wrong in the points it makes. James has his spirituality backwards, inside out, and upside down. How did this book ever get into the Bible? How can we justify leaving it in the canon? Why should we not just tear it out and throw it away? Well, both the sixteenth-century Reformers and the fourth-century Council of the Nicaea almost did. James got into the Bible, despite all of his confusion, because of his simple-minded effort to get one thing across. In the end he did get that point thoroughly worked out in spite of himself, and

Spirituality Upside Down and Inside Out

that point is the point of our text. "Show me your faith without your deeds and I will show you my faith by what I do" (Jas 2:18b). That one important thing he got straight.

Paul says in Eph 2:10, after his great statement of faith in 2:8–9, that "We are God's workmanship, created in Christ Jesus to do good works, which God prepared in advance for us to do." That is, it is clear that we are saved, forgiven, accepted, and eternally secure by grace alone. That is simply an arbitrary act of God that applies to all humans equally. However, mature and healthy faith and trust in that arbitrary act of God express themselves in responsible discipleship. That's what James was struggling so confusedly to get at. The two are radically different from each other and must be kept clear and clean, but James got them all mixed up.

We are God's people because we are chosen by God. The Bible says plainly, "You have not chosen me. I have chosen you" (John 15:16). God did not choose us because we are godly, but in spite of ourselves, because we have no other chance than God's unconditional acceptance of us as we are. We are never under judgment, but always under Grace. We do not *need* to behave godly but we are *invited* to behave godly. Christianity is not an obligation to be labored under but an opportunity to be seized, savored, and celebrated. We are chosen to be God's people and invited or called to act like it. While giving evidence of our saving faith by our godly deeds does not accrue credit for us, nonetheless, we demonstrate our true character and authenticity thereby.

Remember that in the parable of the prodigal son, both brothers end up in the same predicament. The younger brother is the prodigal who runs away and wastes his life. Finally he drags himself back home and pleads for a chance to work hard to prove he really is a nice guy, in spite of himself. His father sets all of that past aside, picks him up and embraces him, puts the royal ring back on his finger in spite of himself, and throws a feast. He says, *My son was dead to me; he is alive again. Nothing else counts* (Luke 15:24, 15:32).

The older brother did everything right all of his life, as any good churchman, but he refused to celebrate his brother's return. Spitting venom through his teeth he angrily assaults his father because the father unconditionally accepts the prodigal son. His father addresses the elder brother, *Well you've got the same problem as your brother. You think I love you because you did everything right and proved your worthiness to me. Actually, I love both of you simply because I am your father, in spite of your behavior.*

Nonetheless, I appreciate your diligence and consequently all I have is yours (Luke 15:30–32).

That sounds all mixed up like James. The father continues, *I love you and your brother because you are my sons. You should not have behaved so well or worked so hard if you thought that I love you because of your good behavior. I would have loved you anyway* (Luke 15:31). That's why Paul can say, *In the end every eye shall see him. Every knee shall bow. Every tongue shall confess that Christ is Lord to the glory of God the Father* (Rom 14:11, Phil 2:10–11). Get yourself ready for it. You are going to find Hitler, Stalin, and Osama bin Laden in heaven despite all the hell they raised. God will be glad you and I were hardworking Christian kingdom-builders, but we will not get any better status in heaven than those poor misguided guys. That is one of the things that is going to make heaven so joyful. We will all notice that God rescued all the awfully flawed persons too. By grace we and they are all saved through faith! That is not of ourselves. It is a gift. In spite of ourselves—a gift! As six feet of earth makes us all the same size, so radical grace puts us all on even ground with God. God rejoices, apparently, when that fact makes us glad to be godly in God's world.

Amen. So let it Be!

SERMON TWENTY SEVEN

So What, Operationally
—Revelations 5:11–14

> I heard a loud voice in heaven say, "Worthy is the Lamb that was slain, to receive power and wealth and wisdom and might and honor and glory and blessing." And I heard those around the throne of God say, "Amen!" Then they all bowed down and worshipped God.
>
> —REVELATION 5:12, 5:14

IN DANIEL 7:13 THERE is a story about a dream-vision in which Daniel saw "one like a son of man" moving on a cloud into the presence of God, the Ancient of Days. It is clear in the vision that this Son of Man is exalted to a heavenly status next to God. He is then given power, authority, and dominion over all the rulers of the earth. His job is to destroy all the evil kingdoms and powers of the earth and to establish in their place the reign of God's justice, grace, and mercy—the kingdom of God on earth. This is to be accomplished through the earthly field forces of the heavenly Son of Man. They are called "The people of the Holy Ones of the Most High" (Dan 7:18, 7:22). That's us folks!

By Grace Alone

Jesus referred to himself exclusively as the Son of Man and indicated that he would be exalted to heaven by God. The first three gospels claimed that after his suffering and death he would be taken up and people would eventually see him return on the clouds of heaven as judge at the end of time. Only John's gospel changes this story to say that he definitely will not return as judge but definitely is the savior of all humanity. He eliminates the wicked by forgiving them: everyone, for everything, for evermore, and he will bring all humanity home to heaven.

The image of the Son of Man resurges in the Book of Revelation. In our text for today, we see the Son of Man as the slain Lamb of God, exalted by God to reign over the kingdom of God throughout the universe. It is not easy to figure out what the author is up to in the Book of Revelation. The entire book is really ridiculous, taken on first look. Like the Epistle of James, Revelation had a difficult time getting into the canon of the Bible because of its weird images and symbols. The Bishops at the Council of Nicaea, where the decision was made as to which books should be included in the Bible, were mostly against Revelation because they thought it such a ridiculous collection of bizarre ideas. It finally made it into the Bible by a margin of one vote because some thought it was written by the apostle John and should be given special consideration.

However, if one understands the situation of the writing of that book it is a bit easier to take. It was written to give the church a triumphalist philosophy of history at the time that the emperor Nero was determined to exterminate the entire Christian movement. When hope seemed almost lost, this book was designed to paint a picture of history in which, against all odds, God would gain a spiritual triumph over all alien forces. God would make this happen by means of the exaltation of the Lamb of God, who was also called the Son of Man, like the man in Daniel 7. The Son of Man was exalted to heaven as the judge of all the earth. The People of the Holy Ones of the Most High would gain the victory over all evil and establish the reign of God throughout the universe.

This philosophy of history did much to support and promote the triumph of the church over the empire, and the conversion of the barbarian hordes to Christianity, as they overran the power of Rome. Revelation provided a Christian myth, composed as a confession of faith, which motivated the Christian community to hope and endurance. There was no historical or theological reality under the myth, but it was an ethereal way of looking at what the church was up against and what desired outcome could

So What, Operationally

be envisioned. The confessional faith-myth became more real than history and functioned as a kind of leaven in the community's life, creating out of thin blue air a future for the church's interpretation of history.

Jack Miles wrote two books about the Bible. The first, on the Old Testament, is *God, a Biography*, and it won the Pulitzer Prize. The second book, the counterpart of the first, treated the New Testament. He called it *Christ: A Crisis in the Life of God*. These are important books. The latter discusses dramatically the way in which the New Testament creates a triumphal faith-story for the church, designed to get it through the tragedies and adversities of history, as it unfolds. It is clear from Jack's book that the story works out quite well, on paper, for God's reputation and for human hopes. It is a great stage drama. The question is, "So what, operationally?" Does it work in real life?

As the Doctor replied to Fibber Magee when he asked about the cost of a medical exam, so also the answer to this operational question is, "That depends!" Whether it works in real life depends upon the quality of one's faith perspective. The quality of one's faith confession determines the quality of one's life. The quality of one's belief produces the quality of one's life. We see and experience life in terms of what we believe, that is, in terms of the nature and quality of our faith-vision. In extremity the quality of our personal faith-myth makes all the difference in the world. Myth, of course, in this context, means one's confession of faith about what is real regarding God and the universe

I know a lot of people whose belief about the way the world is wired and the way Christianity is supposed to operate in it causes them to see everything in life negatively. They live lives of complaint. Others can see nothing but wrong around them. Still others are always full of thoughtless doubt. Then there are those who see everything with great optimism and joyful expectation, almost without exception. It depends upon the quality of their myth, their faith perspective about the way things are. We have each chosen a certain philosophy of life and that is the way we see everything.

Especially in extremity, our quality of life depends completely upon the quality of our myth. The bottom line that informs us of the authenticity and relevance of any faith-visions of any religion is, "Will it bury your child?" Can your personal faith profession about life empower you to stand at the edge of an open grave and let the cold body of your own dead child down into that hole, and still have some kind of life left that is worth living? My father buried three of his own little ones and until his dying day he longed with great and faithful expectation for the day he would see those little ones again. His faith sustained him. It had the nature and quality of faith-vision that endures through thick and thin.

Our text declares, "I heard a loud voice in heaven say, 'Worthy is the Lamb that was slain, to receive power and wealth and wisdom and blessing.' I heard those around the throne of God respond with a resounding, 'Amen!' Then they all bowed down and worshipped God" (Rev 5:12, 5:14). That is a very strange myth. Revelation is full of that kind of wild stuff. If you boil it down to its central message it says, God, in Christ, has triumphed over evil, and God's reign of grace that works and love that heals will be universal.

That myth got the church through Nero's persecution and that of Diocletian, Julian, Constantius, and on and on. Does that myth work for you? Does it fill you with faith in the God of life and of history? Life is about the process of developing your own personal faith-vision which fills your life with meaning and interprets death as an opportunity. Some people really get it. Some get it early. Some never get it until that transitional moment when they pass to eternity and see the Lord face to face. At which point everybody gets it. Every eye sees, every knee bows, and every tongue confesses—to God's joyful triumph!

Amen. So let it Be!

Conclusion

I HAVE SPENT MY professional life preaching sermons and lecturing at universities. I kept one leg in each camp, so to speak. It seemed clear to me that doing so was a calling of the Lord. The work was consistently gratifying and heartening in its fruitfulness. When I look back upon the 60 years of such professional work it is clear to me that both were my divinely revealed vocation, God's clear call to me at age seven. Moreover, keeping one foot in the university and one foot in the pulpit, pastorate, and clinic proved to be a posture in which the two sides of my work mutually enhanced each other. The university kept me up to date. The pastorate and clinic kept me honest to the realities of life down on the ground where, as Toynbee intimated, real life is lived and the significant history is written.

The sermons in this volume are the fruit of those sixty years. They tell my story and in doing so they relate, as clearly as I know how, what I think is God's story in this human world. It is for the reader to decide whether these sermons are as useful, truth-telling, and life-changing as sermons are supposed to be. It is for the Divine Spirit now to empower this modest volume on its way into the minds and hearts of spiritually inquiring readers and preachers whose use of them can potentially multiply my ministry of the Word.

I send them forth with the invitation to anyone who wishes, that they may be used in whatever way they may be effective for the articulation of the gospel's central message of God's radical, unconditional, uncalculating, and universal saving grace, forgiveness and acceptance. "God shows divine love for us in that while we were yet sinners Christ died for us" (Rom 5:8). God is always ahead of the game in the quest for our healing. That is the essence of the good news. I pray that these sermons will be instruments of the Divine Spirit empowering that good news to get loose in our world, so

By Grace Alone

badly in need of it today. Take these messages. Use them as your own. Make them your own. Incarnate them anew. Give them vital new life and vigor. Fill with them the pulpits of the land.

All Hallows Eve, 2012

Index

Abraham, 1, 36ff, 81, 128
Akhenaton, 88
A Distant Mirror, 44
Adultery, 6
Arthur, King, 104
Augustine, St, 141ff

Barth, Karl, 38, 106
Baxter, Richard, 36
Beauty, 14–20
Beecher, Henry Ward, 36
Ben Laden, Osama, 97
Borderline Personality Disorder, 11
Brain, right, left xv, xvi
Bridge Over the River Kwai, 11

Cahill, Thomas, 12, 45
Calvin, John, 52
Cathedral Model Church, 31
Chemistry of Love, 10
Chocolat, 101
Christ, A Crisis in the Life of God, 153ff
Civilisation, 12, 45
Clark, Kenneth, 45
Commission, 34ff
Commitment, 34ff
Constantine, 56, 95, 101
Colonel Bogey March, 11
Covenant, 1, 81, 128
Crotch, 10ff

Death March, 12
De Vries, Peter, 67
Dignity, 12ff

Discipline, 11
Dutch Golden Age, 14

Ecclesiastical Park Model Church, 33
Ellens, Mary Jo, 15
Enron, 17
Erik Erikson, 47
Ethical Capital, 17
Ezra, 106ff

French Existentialism, 2

Genghis Kahn, 97
Gentlemen, 12ff
George III, 46
God, a Biography, 153ff
Good works, 140ff
Gordon, Ernest, 12
Goldwin, Sam, 23
Grace, 1–156
Grant, Ulysses S., 18
Greenberg, Daniel, 19
Greenberg, Roz, 19ff

Hitler, Adolf, 97
Hosea, 66
How the Irish Saved Civilization, 12, 45

Incarnation in preaching xv
Irenaeus, 137

Jerusalem, 110ff
Joseph of Arimathea, 23

Index

Keats, John, 20
Kennedy, John F., 50

Lasch, Christopher, 324
Latimer, Anglican Bishop, xii
Laughing Christ, 64ff
Lewis, C. S., 41
Lewis, E. T., 81
Light, 14ff
Love, 1ff, 31ff
Love and Limmerence, 10

Manners, Good, 10ff
March of Folly, 46
Marriage, 16
Maturity, 6, 33
Merz, Barbara, 87ff
Metaphor, 2ff
Micah, 1ff
Miles, Jack, 153ff
Mission Center Model Church, 32, 33
Montanists, 39
Morality, 16ff
Mortality, 16

Narcissism, 12, 24

O'Connor, Flannery, 67

Panentheist, 93
Parish Model Church, 31
Pascal, Blaise, 127
Pentecost, 37ff, 75
Percy, Walker, 67
Peter, St, 31
Pope John XXIII, 103
Preaching as incarnation, xv
Preaching as oratory (oration), xv
Princeton University Chapel, 12
Prodigal Son, 21
Psychology, xii, xiii, 3, 4, 5, 11

Ravensbruck, 47ff
Red Land, Black Land, 87
Rembrandt, 13–17
Ridley, xii, xiii

Sallman, Warner, 64ff
Schleiermacher, Friedrich, 42, 107ff
Sex, 10, 35
Son of Man, 151ff
Spirit, Divine, Holy xvi–156
Stalin, Joseph, 97
Stary, Stary Night, 15

Tertullian, 39
The Culture of Narcissism, 324
Toynbee, 125
The March of Folly, 46ff
Through the Valley of the Kwai, 12ff
Truth-Teller, 37
Tuchman, Barbara, 44ff

Universal Grace, 1–156
Updike, John, 67
Usscher, Bishop, 29

Van Gogh, Vincent, 15
Vatican II, 60, 103
Vietnam War, 46

Weems, Ann, 48
Wall Street, 17
Washington, George, 17

Yahweh, 1, 128
Young Man Luther, 47

Zacchaeus, 23

www.ingramcontent.com/pod-product-compliance
Lightning Source LLC
Chambersburg PA
CBHW072136160426
43197CB00012B/2134